Alan Hickey is associate producer on the *Postcards* television series so he's in an ideal position to compile this latest collection of stories – the third in the *Postcards* series. As producer he helps select, research and arrange the one hundred or so stories filmed every year. Alan has been in television for more than twenty-five years working on daily news, educational and children's programs, corporate work and now *Postcards*. He also works as a freelance journalist and producer. He lives in Adelaide with his wife, Andrea, and their two children.

Postcards
Day trips from Adelaide

Compiled and edited by Alan Hickey

Written by Alan Hickey, Ron Kandelaars and Keith Conlon

from original television scripts

Wakefield
Press

Wakefield Press
1 The Parade West
Kent Town
South Australia 5067
www.wakefieldpress.com.au
First published 2003
Copyright © Channel 9
South Australia Pty Ltd,
Adelaide, 2003

Designed by Dean Lahn,
Lahn Stafford Design
Typeset by Clinton Ellicott,
Wakefield Press
Printed and bound by
Hyde Park Press

National Library of Australia
Cataloguing-in-publication entry
Hickey, Alan.
Postcards: day trips from
Adelaide.

ISBN 1 86254 626 6.

1. Postcards (Television program).
2. Adelaide Region (S. Aust.) –
Description and travel.
3. Adelaide Region (S. Aust.) –
Guidebooks. I. Conlon, Keith.
II. Kandelaars, Ron. III. Title.

919.4231

Wakefield Press thanks
Fox Creek Wines and
Arts South Australia
for their support.

Curramulka, Yorke Peninsula

Contents

Introduction by Keith Conlon

Photo by Jeff Clayfield

Over the last few years South Australians have developed a real sense of the richness and variety of experiences that are in their own back yard. We hope that this day trip edition of *Postcards* stories strengthens that feeling as we encourage you to join an ever optimistic prospector in his authentic gully gold mine, to glide along a reedy waterway to a winery lunch, to meet the characters who keep the fire burning in an old blacksmith shop, and to get your feet wet as you chase 'big bluey' crabs in the shallows.

We are honoured that Bill Spurr, CEO of the South Australian Tourism Commission, has said publicly that *Postcards* has helped South Australians acquire confidence in their state as a great place to live, work and play. There is one nagging doubt, however, that is sometimes expressed to us: 'Won't you run out of stories?' 'Not on your Nellie!' we reply. South Australia is not a museum piece under glass. Far from it.

This *Postcards* day trip collection helps to dismiss that scurrilous suggestion. Until recently, for instance, you could not taste a family-made prize-winning aged cheddar high on a hill or choose from two dozen lovingly tended individual Barossa wines rarely found in a bottle shop. There were no Kaiki Trail signs to explain a whale pot full of heritage on Granite Island, nor was there a tranquil garden of sacred sculptures in which to find peace. These are all new experiences to beguile visitors from near and far.

On the other hand, visitors could just fall victim to my 'Mona Lisa Theory', namely, that if we didn't know her portrait was 500 years old and painted by Leonardo da Vinci, we might walk straight past it because it's quite small. Similarly, our own 'masterpieces' can be enigmatic and overlooked, but we hope this 'gallery guide' encourages you to stop and enjoy them as much as we have.

So, our thanks again to the passionate enthusiasts who do the hard yakka that makes it easy for the rest of us. See you on the unwinding road.

Editor's Note

One of the strengths of *Postcards* is its consistency – and that's thanks to the people who make up the *Postcards* team on and off camera: Keith Conlon and Jeff Clayfield who have been with the show from day one; producer Ron Kandelaars, and presenter Lisa McAskill. The consistently high production standards are courtesy of Trevor Griscti, Brenda Richards, Brenton Harris, Marc Orrock and Andrew McEvoy. My thanks also to the Royal Automobile Association of SA for their useful maps; the photographers who generously supplied wonderful photos; to Gina Inverarity and Clinton Ellicott from Wakefield Press for their advice and efficiency and Dean Lahn for his great design. Thank you again to all the enthusiastic people who shared their stories with the *Postcards* team for the television program and then assisted with more detail for the book, and thanks to the Tourism officers and staff who supplied information. A special thank you goes to my wonderful wife, Andrea, for her love and support, and my delightful children, Declan and Catherine for their irrepressible spirit.

Alan Hickey

Opposite: from left, Ron Kandelaars,
Lisa McAskill and Keith Conlon
Photo by Jeff Clayfield

Meet the Postcards Team

Having notched up more than three hundred episodes and now entering its ninth year, there's no questioning *Postcards*' position as the premier television showcase for South Australia's remarkable places and faces. At 5.30 pm on Sundays SA tunes in to Channel Nine to see what part of the state Keith and the team have been to and what great yarns they've uncovered.

Postcards is more than just 'pretty pictures'. Sure, there are plenty of them, but it's the stories that really drive *Postcards* – the stories of the people, events and places that make our state of South Australia special.

The extraordinary success of *Postcards* is also reflected in its website. It is a great resource for hundreds of thousands of people seeking information on South Australia. Created by World Wide Architects, www.postcards-sa.com.au often receives some strange requests – like the lady who asked if we knew whether her grandmother had 'played up' while she was living on Wardang Island in the late 1800s. Or the Sydney lady who wanted to know if there was a Holiday Inn at Lake Eyre and whether you can hire a yacht to sail across the lake when it is in flood. Then there's Damien, who wanted to know if we could tell him if his seahorse was pregnant!

The television program, the website and the successful books are all part of the *Postcards* phenomenon.

Adelaide and the Hills

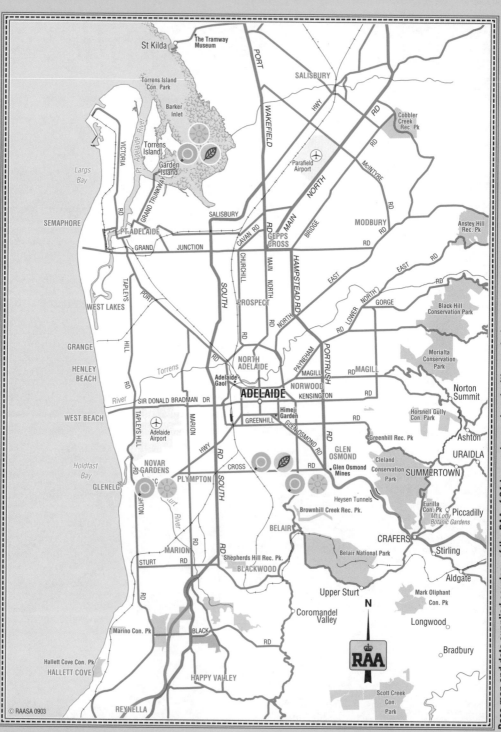

Food/Wine   Walking/Activity   History/Local Interest   Nature/Wildlife

St Kilda
The Tramway Museum
Torrens Island Con. Park
Barker Inlet
PORT
WAKEFIELD
SALISBURY
HWY
RD
Cobbler Creek Rec. Pk.
Parafield Airport
Largs Bay
Torrens Island
Garden Island
NORTH
Anstey Hill Rec. Pk.
MAIN
McINTYRE
RD
RD
VICTORIA
Pt ADELAIDE River
GRAND TRUNKWAY
SALISBURY
SEMAPHORE
PT ADELAIDE
CAVAN RD
RD
GEPPS CROSS
MAIN NORTH
BRIDGE
MODBURY
RD
Anstey Hill Rec. Pk.
GRAND
JUNCTION
CHURCHILL
PROSPECT
HAMPSTEAD RD
EAST
EAST
RD
Black Hill Conservation Park
TAPLEYS
PORT
SOUTH
RD
NORTH
RD
LOWER NORTH
GORGE
Morialta Conservation Park
WEST LAKES
GRANGE
HENLEY BEACH
Torrens
NORTH ADELAIDE
Adelaide Gaol
PAYNEHAM
PORTRUSH
MAGILL
MAGILL
RD
Norton Summit
RD
HILL
RD
ADELAIDE
NORWOOD
KENSINGTON
RD
WEST BEACH
River
SIR DONALD BRADMAN DR
GREENHILL
Himeji Garden
Horsnell Gully Con. Pk
Ashton
MARION
Adelaide Airport
TAPLEYS HILL
HWY
RD
GREENHILL
RD
GLENOSMOND RD
RD
Greenhill Rec. Pk
URAIDLA
Holdfast Bay
NOVAR GARDENS
CROSS
SOUTH
RD
GLEN OSMOND
Glen Osmond Mines
Cleland Conservation Park
SUMMERTOWN
GLENELG
PLYMPTON
Heysen Tunnels
Eurilla Con. Pk
Piccadilly
Mt Lofty Botanic Gardens
Brownhill Creek Rec. Pk.
RD
MARION
STURT
RD
BELAIR
CRAFERS
Stirling
Shepherds Hill Rec. Pk.
Belair National Park
BLACKWOOD
RD
Aldgate
Upper Sturt
Mark Oliphant Con. Pk
Marino Con. Pk
BLACK
Coromandel Valley
Longwood
Hallett Cove Con. Pk
HALLETT COVE
RD
Bradbury
HAPPY VALLEY
N
RAA
Scott Creek Con. Park
REYNELLA

© RAASA 0903

City skyline, Adelaide

To Saunders Gorge
(See River Murray Map)
BIRDWOOD

Inglewood

HOUGHTON

GUMERACHA

Paracombe

Cudlee
Creek

MT
TORRENS

Black Hill
Conservation
Park

Montacute
Con. Pk

Mt Crawford Forest

Morialta
Conservation
Park

Norton
Summit

Cherryville

Lobethal

Marble Hill

ADELAIDE

Horsnell Gully
Con. Pk

Greenhill
Rec. Pk

Ashton

Basket
Range

Lenswood

Charleston

A17

Cleland
Con. Park

SUMMERTOWN

URAIDLA

Woodside

Harrogate

Kenneth Sterling
Conservation Park

Brownhill Creek
Rec. Pk

Cleland
Wildlife
Park

Mt Lofty Summit
Eurilla Con. Pk

Piccadilly

Kenneth
Sterling
Con. Park

Mt Lofty
Botanic Garden

Mt George
Con. Pk

BALHANNAH

Oakbank

Brukunga

CRAFERS

Wittunga
Botanic
Gardens

Belair National Park

Stirling

S.E.

Verdun

Blackwood

Aldgate

Heathfield

BRIDGE-
WATER

Hahndorf

Nairne

Blackwood
Forest
Rec. Park

Upper
Sturt

Mark Oliphant
Con. Pk

M1

Hahndorf
Farm Barn

Littlehampton

Coromandel
Valley

Longwood

Mylor

River

Totness
Rec. Pk

FWY

M1

Bradbury

Onkaparinga

MT BARKER

Kanmantoo

Scott Creek
Con.
Park

ECHUNGA

Wistow

Clarendon

Kuitpo
Forest

Flaxley

Kangarilla

MACCLESFIELD

Kuitpo Forest

MEADOWS

Woodchester

N

Prospect
Hill

RAA

Kuitpo Forest

Kyeema
Con. Pk

Strathalbyn

Ashbourne

Mt Magnificent
Con. Pk

© RAASA 0903

Adelaide skyline

t is difficult to separate the city of Adelaide from the magnificent backdrop of the Adelaide Hills. Ride the lift up any high building in the city and you'll feast on a view of thousands of trees and hectares of parklands for which Adelaide has become famous. And the leafy view to the east is continued beyond the city into the magnificent Mount Lofty Ranges.

Where else can you take a twenty-minute drive from the city centre and end up among thick Aussie bush shrouding a varied collection of historical villages? Adelaide and its Hills have a lot in common. The city has the grace and charm of a modern metropolis but it has managed to retain its history through its grand buildings and architecture. The Hills too has an eclectic mix of past and present. The modern Heysen Tunnels on the South Eastern Freeway take us past architecturally designed houses clinging to the hills face into towns and villages full of early European history.

It's easy, in fact almost compulsory, to spend a day exploring the city and another day in the Hills. From Adelaide's endless suburban beaches to the iconic Central Market, Adelaide Oval, Tandanya, the Museum, Art Gallery, Botanic Garden or sailing the Torrens Lake on *Popeye* – there's more than enough to keep you occupied.

A drive through the Hills will take you through scenery that constantly changes from thick bush, rolling vineyards and orchards to lush farmland. Taste Hahndorf's German heritage, cuddle a koala at Cleland Wildlife Park or get into our motoring past at Birdwood's National Motor Museum. You won't do it all in a day – but that's part of the attraction.

Tips from the Crew

• Ron says you'll see the Australian bush through different eyes after visiting Hans Heysen's former home and studio, The Cedars at Hahndorf. Then you can take a stroll along part of the famous walking trail named in his honour.

• Keith says a visit to the Mount Lofty Botanic Garden is great any time but spectacular in autumn – the deciduous colours are stunning. Remember to take a pen and paper to jot down the names of your favourite trees.

• If you have the need for speed Lisa recommends touching down at the Classic Jet Fighter Museum at Parafield Airport. It's crammed with jet aircraft used by the Royal Australian Airforce and the Navy from the 1950s right through to 1980.

• If you're looking for a game of beach volleyball you don't have to go to the beach. Trevor says you should head to City Beach on the corner of Frome Road and Pirie Street. The courts are open daily from 9 a.m.

• The RAA has been helping motorists for over 100 years. To see how it all began Lisa

Bushwalking, Mawson Trail, Lenswood, Adelaide Hills

Want More Information?

SA Visitor and Travel Centre
1300 655 276

Port Adelaide Visitor Centre
(08) 8405 6560

Glenelg Visitor Centre
(08) 8294 5833

Adelaide Passenger Transport
(08) 8210 1000

Adelaide Hills Visitor Information Centre
1800 353 323

Adelaide Hills website
www.visitadelaidehills.com.au

National Parks and Wildlife SA
(08) 8204 1910

RAA Touring (maps and guides)
(08) 8202 4600

SA Tourism Commission website
www.southaustralia.com

***Postcards* website**
www.postcards-sa.com.au

---

suggests a visit to the RAA Museum which is part of the customer centre on Richmond Road, Mile End.

• If you enjoy 'thinking big' Jeff reckons you should head to the wooden toy factory at Gumeracha. It's home to the biggest rocking horse in the world – it's more than 18 metres high.

I Didn't Know That

• *Popeye* has been gliding along the Torrens for a long time. The first *Popeye* was built on the banks of the river by Harold Lounder in 1935.

• The Bicentennial Conservatory in the Adelaide Botanic Garden is the largest greenhouse in the southern hemisphere.

• The foundation stone of the Adelaide Town Hall was laid on 4 May 1863 after the Corporation of Adelaide paid twelve shillings for the one-acre piece of land. The price of a gentlemen's ticket to the opening night ball was twice the price.

• Australia's first police force was set up in South Australia by Governor Gawler in 1838.

Top Attractions

Adelaide Hills

The Cedars – 1 kilometre out of Hahndorf

Hans Heysen's historic home is nestled among the majestic gum trees which featured in many of his paintings. Take a step back in time and wander through the gardens or take a guided tour.

Cleland Wildlife Park – Mount Lofty

Come face to face with some of Australia's unusual birds, animals and reptiles. Aboriginal guides bring Dreaming stories to life.

National Motor Museum – Birdwood

There are over 300 cars, motorbikes and commercial vehicles on display here along with exhibitions, interactive fun for kids, barbeques and picnic grounds.

Hahndorf Farm Barn – 2 kilometres out of Hahndorf

Heaps of fun for the family. Bottle-feed the animals, cuddle the guinea pigs and rabbits. There's daily sheep shearing and hand milking of Daisy the cow.

Warrawong Earth Sanctuary – Mylor

A haven for rare and endangered wildlife. Enjoy the acclaimed dawn, day and dusk sanctuary tours, Indigenous cultural interpretation, unique accommodation and Australian cuisine in the restaurant.

Gorge Wildlife Park – Cudlee Creek

Australia's largest privately owned collection of animals and birds contained in five-and-a-half hectares of natural bushland. Walk through aviaries, see monkeys, mountain lions, leopards and of course Australian wildlife.

Mount Lofty Botanic Garden – Mount Lofty

Several walking trails take visitors up and down seven valleys, each dedicated to a particular plant group. There are stunning massed displays of rhododendrons, roses, camellias and peonies against a backdrop of native stringybark forest.

Mount Lofty Summit – Mount Lofty

See the ever-changing views of Adelaide and its coastline from 710 metres above sea level. There's tourist information, souvenirs and top-quality food at the fully licensed restaurant.

Adelaide

Adelaide Botanic Garden – North Terrace

Opened in 1857 and featuring a glorious Victorian garden landscape which includes avenues of mature trees, particularly Araucaria and Morton Bay figs, and important garden buildings like the Museum of Economic Botany and the historic Palm House.

Adelaide Central Market – Grote Street

Always busy, colourful and aromatic the Central Market has the biggest range of fresh food and produce in the southern hemisphere.

Adelaide Festival Centre – King William Road

The centre has hosted many world famous performances and is the home of the Adelaide Festival. The backstage tour is a must.

Adelaide Zoological Gardens – Frome Road

In the heart of Adelaide this is the place to see and learn about the world's rare and endangered animals.

Tandanya – Grenfell Street

The National Aboriginal Cultural Institute promotes understanding and appreciation of Aboriginal cultures through changing exhibitions, guided tours and performances.

Adelaide Hills
Settlement Museum
at Hahndorf

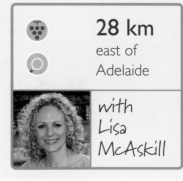

28 km
east of
Adelaide

with
Lisa
McAskill

There's nothing quite like ambling through Ambleside, which is what Hahndorf was called when anti-German sentiment ran high during World War I. The name was changed by an Act of Parliament in 1917 but thankfully, when emotions cooled, it reverted to Hahndorf, the name the town was given in memory of Captain Dirk Hahn, who brought some of the first German settlers to South Australia in the 1840s.

The charming hills town is now Australia's oldest surviving German settlement and one of the most visited places in South Australia.

A casual wander around Hahndorf and its neighbouring villages reveal some wonderful glimpses of the area's early history. But it's easy to become confused by the many different stories of early settlement and the old barns, farmhouses and flourmills scattered throughout the towns and villages. That's where the Adelaide Hills Settlement Museum at Hahndorf comes in. Step inside and the amazing feats of the men and women who settled the area become clear. Local historian Gordon Young has a deep

Adelaide Hills Settlement Museum incorporates the cellar door for Mawson Ridge Wines Photo by Madeleine Marin

Local produce and handicraft add to
the experience Photo by Madeleine Marin

respect for the Germans of Hahndorf, the Scots of Oakbank and all the other pioneers who opened up the Hills. 'They came from all over,' explained Gordon. 'And they brought with them their own ways of building.'

To help us make sense of it all, the museum shows a film which explains the various building styles and their uses. It makes a drive through the historic precincts of the Hills so much more enjoyable – once you know what you're looking for! For example, it points you in the direction of hidden treasures like the original church at Lobethal, which is said to be the oldest Lutheran church in Australia. There are also stories about how some of today's popular watering holes have evolved from homesteads into country pubs.

Local history isn't the only thing on offer at the Museum as it's also a showcase for local wine and produce. The shop-front is the cellar door outlet for Mawson Ridge Wines which means that between the history lessons you can taste some wine and stock up on locally made conserves, jams, olive oil and honey.

Mawson Ridge vignerons Madeleine and Raymond Marin say they chose the main street of Hahndorf because of the links between the history of fine wine and the early settlement. 'What better place to show off the history, architecture and local produce of the Adelaide Hills?' Madeleine asked.

It's a fine blend well overdue.

24 Main Street, Hahndorf
South Australia 5245
incorporating Mawson Ridge Wines
Cellar door sales, wine tasting
and local produce
Tel (08) 8388 1288
Open Tuesday to Sunday
September to June,
Wednesday to Sunday
July to August

Adelaide Hills
Settlement
Museum

Canoeing through the Garden Island Ships' Graveyard

18 km
north of
Adelaide

with
Ron
Kandelaars

Experience the wrecks up close

Photo by Brenda Richards

Early morning and the *Postcards* team has joined a group from the Adelaide Canoe Club gently paddling along the North Arm of the Port River. It's hard to believe that Gepps Cross and Pooraka are just a few kilometres away as we approach an opening in the thick wall of mangroves.

Our leader, David Mallett, smiled as he explained that canoes can reach a lot of places motor boats can't get to. He even pointed out a channel that leads as far as the salt fields on Main North Road.

We glided almost silently among the thick mangroves and became consumed by the beauty and mystery of the shallows. The mangroves are fascinating examples of adaptation – they survive the constant rise and fall of the tide by breathing through spikes sent up through the mud.

Soon, like the mangroves at low tide, I too was sucking in the oxygen as my fellow paddlers set a cracking pace steering towards one of the Port River's most popular but eerie attractions. At the southern end of Garden Island is one of the biggest ships' grave-yards in the world – the resting ground for a collection of sailing ships, steamers, ferries and barges dating back to 1856.

It wasn't long before the first ship skeleton came into view – the rusting hulk of the *Santiago*. Built in Scotland in 1856, she worked the trade routes between Britain and South America. She was brought to Australia and used as a coal ship at the turn of the century but her trading life came to an end here when she was scuttled in 1945. 'She's the oldest and the last of the twenty-four wrecks to be scuttled here,' explained David. 'She's starting to break up too – the stern section has already dropped away.'

You can paddle right up to the 24 wrecks scuttled here Photo by Brenda Richards

The beauty of this tour is that you paddle through the very heart of South Australian maritime history. At one stage we cruised through the half-submerged hull of the *Dorothy H. Sterling*. A six-masted schooner built in Portland, USA, in 1920, only part of her solid timber frame remains. During the Depression locals stripped her precious oregon hull for firewood. And as David points out, now nature is stripping away what remains. 'The mangroves have started colonising the wreck and they'll gradually fill her up. Eventually, she'll be completely taken over.'

But that'll take a few years so there's plenty of time to visit the Garden Island Ships' Graveyard. It's a regular haunt for the enthusiasts who make up the Adelaide Canoe Club and you never know, you might be as lucky as we were and have a couple of dolphins escort you part of the way.

Canoe SA
PO Box 281, Port Adelaide
South Australia 5015
Tel (08) 8240 3294
Canoes available for hire

Adelaide
Canoe Club

Historic Cummins House

7 km
south-west
of Adelaide

with
Keith
Conlon

Historic Cummins House has some striking claims to fame. It was built with locally fired red bricks in 1842 by Sir John Morphett, a man of great influence in the early days of South Australia.

Surrounded by suburbia now the house used to be the centrepiece of a 134 acre farm. It stands perched on a sandhill next to the Sturt River on land selected by Sir John. He had plenty of opportunity to make his choice too – as an agent for the South Australian Company, he arrived from England just a few weeks after Colonel William Light.

No doubt Sir John strode along the wide brick terrace and elaborate porch as he contemplated his ongoing role in the settlement's growth. He and his wife, Elizabeth, would have been pleased with their morning room too. The views stretched over the swampy lowlands along the Sturt River to the foothills. A 1936 Centenary hooked rug hangs on the wall depicting Proclamation under the Old Gum Tree at Glenelg. Quite appropriate really because the Morphetts were there – Elizabeth came out on HMS *Buffalo*.

A sweeping driveway leads to the grand house　　　The drawing room exudes opulence　　Photos by Keith Miller

Some of the original furniture remains in the house so the lofty grand dining room, with its beautiful bay window and long cedar table, looks much as it did 150 years ago. We can imagine the conversations over dinner as Morphett led the campaign for a monument over Light's grave in Light Square.

The drawing room is unusual for its time – circular in shape it protrudes into the surrounding garden and is lit by tall and slightly curved windows. Only the best brocade would do for the circular ottoman, and the rich gold and chocolate design of the carpet was specially woven for the house.

Where does one shop to decorate a room like this? London, of course! Mrs Morphett headed off by ship, taking ten children and two servants with her. Money was no object, especially after Sir John added to his fortune during the copper bonanza at Burra.

There's still a sense of the family and the personal in Cummins House. Photos show the eleven Morphett children playing in the creek under the old bridge that their father used to cross on his daily ride. Morphett loved horses – he gave his name to Morphettville Racecourse and was a founder of the South Australian Jockey Club.

After being the family home to five generations of the Morphett family, Cummins House is now owned by the State Government and, thanks to a band of committed volunteers, we can all now enjoy both the house and the acre or so of beautiful gardens. There are pretty locations inside and out for wedding ceremonies and it is open on the first and third Sunday of each month as a museum. The modest entry fee includes Devonshire tea. It certainly lives up to its name, Historic Cummins House.

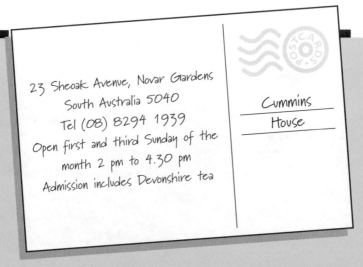

23 Sheoak Avenue, Novar Gardens
South Australia 5040
Tel (08) 8294 1939
Open first and third Sunday of the
month 2 pm to 4.30 pm
Admission includes Devonshire tea

Cummins
House

The Sacred Garden

7 km
south-east
of Adelaide

with
Lisa
McAskill

Adelaide is renowned for its parks and gardens but look closely in the foothills at Glen Osmond and you'll find a very special place. Set within the grounds of the Passionist Catholic Monastery on Cross Road is a place of contemplation known as the Sacred Garden.

The garden features fourteen magnificent marble sculptures depicting Christ's final moments through the Stations of the Cross. They come from the workshop of Franco Miozza of Pietrasanta in Tuscany, the home of Carrara marble and the source of Michelangelo's *David*. Each station is made up of three or four half-size figures and weighs half a ton. The anatomical detail of each figure is almost perfect and to think they were carved from one solid piece of marble is amazing.

Each sculpture weighs half a ton

The sculptures are carved from famous Carrara marble

The stations tell the story of Christ's final hours up to his crucifixion and burial but you don't need to be religious to appreciate their grace and beauty. Look out for the fine detail in the base of some of the stations where the artists have left little signature pieces such as tiny exquisitely crafted flowers. They show that even in the worst of times there are moments of beauty. And according to the Monastery's team that's why the Garden is here.

The Sacred Garden is open daily and is on the southern side of the Monastery at 15 Cross Road, Glen Osmond.

15 Cross Road, Glen Osmond
South Australia 5064
Open daily 9 am to 5 pm

The
Sacred
Garden

Saunders Gorge Sanctuary

81 km east of Adelaide

with Ron Kandelaars

A spectacular gorge reminiscent of the magnificent Flinders Ranges that doesn't take most of the day to reach? Yes, it does exist and it's only ninety minutes from the Adelaide GPO. Saunders Gorge is eighteen kilometres east of Mount Pleasant and it's one of a series of gorges which cut their way through the drier eastern portions of the Mount Lofty Ranges.

You won't see any yellow-footed rock wallabies but you will come across plenty of kangaroos and other wildlife because the rugged Saunders Gorge is actually part of a 1300 hectare private sanctuary owned and operated by Brenton and Nadene Newman.

As we got out of Brenton's four-wheel-drive and headed into the spectacular gorge on foot he told us that it used to be part of the Clovelly Sheep Station. 'This is the rugged eastern side of the Mount Lofty Ranges. That means we get substantially less rainfall than other parts of the Ranges.'

I was struck by the similarities to the Flinders Ranges. 'The climate is not that much different to the Flinders Ranges,' explained Brenton. 'As a result, we've actually got remnants of Flinders type vegetation on the eastern slopes.'

Outcrops of yakkas line the gorge and during a flash flood Brenton reckons you'd swear you were closer to Wilpena than Walker Flat. The huge rocks and boulders have been worn down by thousands of years of water flowing through the gorge. The process is continuing; during thunderstorms massive amounts of water charge through here, further eroding the rocks.

It's not the Flinders Ranges and it's only 90 minutes from Adelaide Photo by Brenton Newman

The nature lodges are ideal for a near-outback experience Photo by Brenton Newman

The wildlife is stunning too thanks to an abundant supply of underground water. 'Even during a very dry summer there's a touch of green in Saunders Gorge,' Brenton said, 'and with the underground water comes the wildlife.' The day we were there we saw a variety of birds including the white winged chuff – a family-orientated bird that lives in flocks and makes its nest from mud scooped from the nearby waterholes.

The chuffs are a bit like Brenton – territorial, and with no intention of leaving. His family moved here forty years ago and he's keen to share his back yard with others. He and Nadene have built a collection of huts and nature lodges that are ideal bases from which to explore Saunders Gorge. There's even a 120-year-old farm cottage, a reminder of the area's early sheep grazing history.

It's a great place for a family to get a near-city outback experience. Late afternoon is the ideal time to explore Saunders Gorge and if you've booked in for the night it's a good idea to get up early and head off on the dawn patrol.

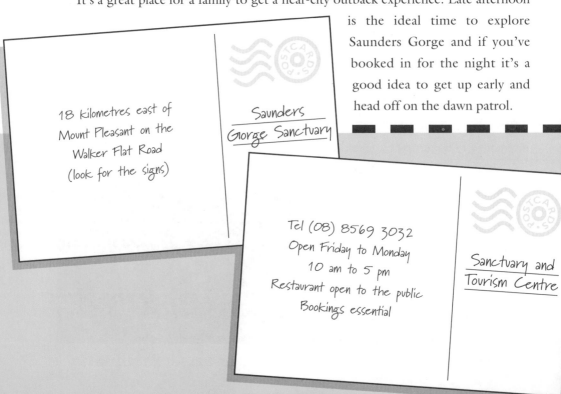

18 kilometres east of Mount Pleasant on the Walker Flat Road (look for the signs)

Saunders Gorge Sanctuary

Tel (08) 8569 3032
Open Friday to Monday
10 am to 5 pm
Restaurant open to the public
Bookings essential

Sanctuary and Tourism Centre

Strathalbyn – SA's Antique Capital

☀ **52 km** south-east of Adelaide

with Keith Conlon

Strathalbyn is a classified Heritage Town that boasts two main streets – one on each side of the Angas River. Its shopping and business focus is on Dawson Street while across the river and park there's High Street with its collection of antiques and curios stores.

To explore this attractive town properly our first stop was at the picturesque railway station that houses the Visitor Information Centre. Equipped with a heritage walk map I set out to explore some of the 30 buildings of interest. I passed the old gasworks (now a beautifully restored bed and breakfast) and the old court house and police station in Rankine Street which houses the National Trust Museum, and headed to the green reserve on the horseshoe bend in the Angas in the centre of town.

It's now the Soldiers Memorial Park, complete with a quaint Edwardian iron rotunda, but markings on some river red gums further along show it was originally part of the Ngarrindjeri nation. In 1839 a group of hardy Scots led by the Rankine family from Ayreshire arrived after five months at sea. They camped on the big bend, built the town and eventually named it 'strath' for a valley with a river and 'albyn' for the mines in Scotland.

The park is dominated by a distinctive arched footbridge over the river called the Children's Bridge. It was built and named by a district farmer in memory of his wife who died childless in the early 1900s. Today the bridge is a prime viewing spot for the annual duck race held every November when the Rotary Club launches 2500 yellow plastic ducks on the river. It creates much merriment for the picnic day hordes and raises money for charity.

Look out for the old two-storey Argus Newspaper building on Commercial Road just above the river. The *Southern Argus* was South Australia's first rural newspaper. The building now houses a colourful craft shop and gives a taste of what's to come on our ramble around town.

The children's bridge over the Angas River and, right, the Soldiers' Memorial Gardens   Photos by Peter Fergusson

On the other side of the river we wander into the 'other' main street – High Street – and meet up with Strathalbyn's legendary town crier, Mac O'Donnell. Mac's motto is 'have bell, will travel' and he'll climb aboard your tour bus any day and tell you tales of the town. The day we were there he was spruiking about the annual gathering of the antique and craft clan that take over the town in August each year.

There is a year-round concentration of dealers in the well-preserved nineteenth-century High Street. 'All in Good Time Antiques' operates out of an old blacksmith shop and specialises in immaculate scientific instruments, old signs and antique furniture. There was a relaxing feel about the place during our visit – a stark contrast to its black-smith days because the two-storey general store 'London House' just up the street was a stagecoach stop in the gold rush days. The Hill and Co. horses were kept in the old stone stables that are still out the back. Built in 1867, London House is a stalwart in the campaign to make Strathalbyn the antiques town of South Australia.

Further along High Street there are plenty more heritage shops like the old pharmacy which houses 'Highlander Antiques'. Its numerous rooms are beautifully dressed in quality furniture, crockery, silverware and all the accoutrements of high Victorian domestic bliss.

We found a real surprise in the old carpenter's shop just around the corner. A virtuoso didgeridoo performance might be unusual enough, but what's a very blond German immigrant named Hermann doing playing and selling them amongst his antiques, bric-a-brac and books? That's another story, and you'll have to pop in and ask.

More typical of the mainstream is the expansive Antique Market opposite the Commercial Hotel. A dozen or more small traders share the space to pursue their enjoyment of the romance and workmanship of the past.

Having a yarn with Mac, the town crier Photo by Peter Fergusson   Main street, Strath

The market adds colour and variety to the High Street which also offers crafts, collectables, handmade teddy bears, beautifully sewn heirlooms of the future and one of the biggest collections of 'Depression glass' I've seen.

Of course, any self-respecting High Street has its own lolly shop – just the spot to gather some goodies for the trip home. Strathalbyn is a town that is high on the day trip list any time of the year, but remember the Antique and Craft Fair held every August. More than sixty traders from near and far present their best and there's even a shuttle bus to take you around. The rest of the time Strath is a pretty heritage town that really is South Australia's antique capital.

South Terrace, Strathalbyn
South Australia 5255
Tel (08) 8536 3212
Open Monday to Friday
9 am to 5 pm, weekend and
public holidays 10 pm to 4 pm
Email info@strathalbyntourism.com.au

Strathalbyn
Visitor
Information
Centre

Third weekend of August each year
Contact Fair Convener
(08) 8536 4077

Strathalbyn
Collectors,
Hobbies and
Antique Fair

Urrbrae House and Arboretum

6 km
south-east of
Adelaide

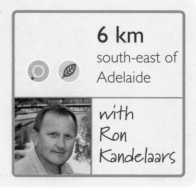

*with
Ron
Kandelaars*

Adelaide has its share of grand and stately homes. The city is punctuated with impressive mansions and all have their own story. The same is true of Urrbrae House off Fullarton Road, which holds pride of place in what was once a sprawling estate.

The house is one of the legacies of Peter Waite who left the small Scottish town of

Kirkcaldy in 1859 and settled in the mid north of the young colony of South Australia. His innovative management of pastoral properties was very successful and lead him to form a business partnership with Thomas Elder and Robert Barr Smith who together founded Elder Smith. Waite became fabulously wealthy and by the 1870s he and his family returned to Adelaide and built Urrbrae House.

A visit today shows how much of an innovator Peter Waite really was. Urrbrae was the first private residence in Adelaide to have electric lights. And to prove he was a real gadgets man, you can walk inside Australia's first domestic refrigeration plant. It might look like a sauna but it's really a fridge, complete with ammonia compressor and fan.

When he died in 1922, Peter Waite bequeathed it all to the University of Adelaide and the Waite Agricultural Research Institute was formed. Now the house is open to the public, free of charge, on the first Sunday of each month.

Urrbrae House was once the centrepiece of a sprawling estate

The Arboretum covers 30 hectares

As you enter off Fullarton Road you'll drive through the spectacular Arboretum – another of Waite's legacies. It covers 30 hectares and contains over 2000 tree specimens from all over the world, all of which grow under natural rainfall. The aim was to see how they do in Adelaide's climate. The Arboretum's formal avenue is one of the most impressive in the state. The long rows of elms were planted in 1928, six years after Peter Waite's death. It all stands as part of a giant, living and growing experiment in the suburbs of Adelaide.

The first Sunday of each month is the time to visit. Free tours of the Arboretum leave from Urrbrae House at eleven o'clock. After lunch guides will take you on a tour of the house at two o'clock.

Off Fullarton Road
Open first Sunday of month,
tours begin at 2 pm
Contact Urrbrae House
(08) 8303 7497

Urrbrae House

Off Fullarton Road
Open daily
Free guided walks
on first Sunday of month,
meet outside Urrbrae House
at 11 am

Waite
Arboretum

Barossa Valley

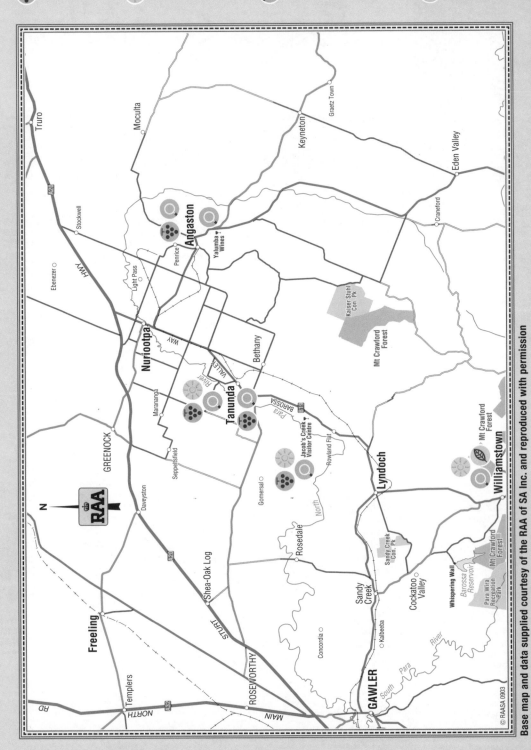

Food/Wine   Walking/Activity   History/Local Interest   Nature/Wildlife

Truro
Mocutta
Graetz Town
Keyneton
Eden Valley
Stockwell
Craneford
HWY
A20
Ebenezer
Light Pass
Penrice
Angaston
Yalumba Wines
Kaiser Stuhl Con. Pk
Mt Crawford Forest
Nuriootpa
WAY
Bethany
Marananga
River
BAROSSA VALLEY
Tanunda
Para
Jacob's Creek Visitor Centre
Rowland Flat
Mt Crawford Forest
GREENOCK
A20
Seppeltsfield
Gomersal
North
Williamstown
Daveyston
RAA
N
Rosedale
Sandy Creek Con. Pk
Whispering Wall
Barossa Reservoir
Mt Crawford Forest
Para Wirra Recreation Park
Shea-Oak Log
Lyndoch
Sandy Creek
Cockatoo Valley
Freeling
STURT
Concordia
Kalbeeba
Templers
ROSEWORTHY
South Para
River
NORTH
RD
MAIN
A32
GAWLER

© RAASA 0903

Base map and data supplied courtesy of the RAA of SA Inc. and reproduced with permission

Vineyards, Eden Valley, Barossa

There are 30 churches scattered throughout the valley

It might be world renowned for its fine wine but there's more to the Barossa Valley than viticulture. Perched conveniently on Adelaide's doorstep the Valley epitomises the 'SA in a day' experience. Within an hour's easy drive, the Barossa is a patchwork of rolling vines, rocky outcrops and red-gum-studded pastures.

Of course there are the famous wineries, big and small, but to really sample Valley life make time for the delightful towns and villages that punctuate the scenery. They reflect the rich history of the hard-working free settlers and Germans who moved into the area from the 1830s. The small village of Bethany near Tanunda is the site of the first German settlement in 1842 and, thankfully, it has preserved many good examples of early East German peasant architecture. In contrast, the town of Angaston is often described as the British corner of the Barossa with its gracious tree-lined main street of fine buildings.

The hard work and determination of the early folk have created a culture unique in the Barossa. It was important to be self sufficient so the art of preserving food was refined. As a result the locals are masters at smoking meats and making cheese, bread and wine. Today, the legacy is the Barossa's special blend of food, hospitality, festivals, walking trails and heritage – all of which are as good as the wines it produces.

Tips from the Crew

• Lisa suggests following the Butcher, Baker, Winemaker Trail to taste the Barossa's distinctive regional food. Pick up a copy of the brochure from the Barossa Wine and Visitor Information Centre in Tanunda.

• The Seppelt family mausoleum on Seppeltsfield Road is difficult to miss. It is styled like a Greek Doric Temple and dominates the hillside. The climb to the top is worth it for the views across the valley. Continue on to Seppelt Winery.

• Ron says if the kids get tired of visiting the wineries take them to the Story Book Cottage and Whacky Wood in Tanunda.

The Cottage has displays of dozens of children's fairytales and nursery rhymes while Whacky Wood has Australian crazy games and puzzles.

• If you are into walking or bike riding, Brenda reckons you are well looked after in this region. The Heysen Walking Trail and the Mawson Cycling Trail take in part of the Barossa Ranges.

Top Attractions

Mengler Hill Lookout – 8 kilometres from Tanunda

Get a spectacular panoramic view of the Barossa Valley and its surrounds. There's also a Sculpture Park with works carved from marble, granite and 'black granite'.

Town Walks

Bethany, Tanunda and Angaston have heritage town walking trails. Pick up a brochure from the Barossa Wine and Visitor Information Centre at Tanunda.

Barossa Wine Centre – Murray Street, Tanunda

Australia's first wine interpretive centre tells the complete Barossa story.

It explores the history, people and culture of the valley and explains the journey from vine to wine.

Whispering Wall – Cockatoo Valley

The kids will love this one – the curved dam holding back the Barossa Reservoir is an acoustic marvel. A message 'whispered' on one side of the wall can be clearly heard on the other side – 140 metres away!

Luhr's Cottage – Light Pass

In 1848 Johann Heinrich Luhr, the first Lutheran school teacher at Light Pass, built a pug cottage. A visit to the cottage and garden is a classic slice of German culture.

Barossa Goldfields Trail – Cockatoo Valley

A fascinating insight into the Barossa's booming gold rush in the late 1860s when ten thousand people descended on the Valley in the hope of finding their fortunes. There are two well sign-posted walking trails. Pick up a brochure from the Barossa Wine and Visitor Information Centre in Tanunda.

Want More Information?

SA Visitor and Travel Centre
1300 655 276

Barossa Wine and Visitor Centre
66–68 Murray Street, Tanunda
1300 852 982

Barossa Valley website
www.barossa-region.org

Gawler Visitor Centre
(08) 8522 6814

National Parks and Wildlife SA
(08) 8280 7048

RAA Touring (maps and guides)
(08) 8202 4600

SA Tourism Commission website
www.southaustralia.com

***Postcards* website**
www.postcards-sa.com.au

I Didn't Know That

- While the English settlers chose the hills around Angaston and Eden Valley, the Lutherans preferred the valley floor. There are about 30 churches, mostly Lutheran, built of local stone, scattered throughout the Barossa.

- Nuriootpa is the Barossa Valley's largest town. Its name comes from a local Aboriginal word 'nguriatpa' meaning 'a meeting place'.

- Angaston is 92 metres above the floor of the valley. It is the highest part of the Barossa at 361 metres above sea level.

- Lyndoch was named by Colonel William Light in honour of his friend, Lord Lynedoch. Light served under Lynedoch at the Battle of Barrosa in Spain. Just as Barrosa became Barossa, Lynedoch was misspelt in South Australia and became Lyndoch.

- The rose bushes planted at the end of rows of vines in a lot of vineyards serve as an early warning sign of fungal diseases.

Barossa Farmers' Market

84 km
north-east
of Adelaide

with
Keith
Conlon

Get up early on any Saturday morning and head to the Vintner's Shed near Angaston and you'll be rewarded with a special slice of Barossa Valley life. The Barossa Farmers' Market is full of passionate personalities, regional character, the colours of the seasons and real food.

Inside the barrel-maturation shed you can savour the concentrated flavour of food and produce from the farms and home kitchens of the Valley. But you need to be quick – among the early sell-outs the morning we made the effort were strawberry tarts from Netherhill and Lyndoch Bakery's pretzels. After an hour, a display fridge earlier laden with sumptuous fruit tarts and quiches was cleaned out. The stall is cheekily nick-named 'The Old Tart', which local chef Barbara bears with a grin.

You need to be early because the market sells out fast Photo by Michael Collet

Plenty of home-made produce   Photo by Michael Collet

The market is also very much about freshly and locally picked fruit and vegetables. I saw plenty of the regulars leaving with baskets overflowing with greens and golden pumpkins.

'What are these like?' I asked, dipping into a sample dish of pickled cucumber slices. 'They should taste good, I've been making them for 30 years,' came the cheery reply.

In another aisle Rosie brings in eggs fresh from her farm where 2500 hens roam free, and her cheeky mate, Keith, reckons she knows them all by name: 'Chook, Chook, Chook!' There's plenty of hot food to tempt the tastebuds with a number of local chefs cooking up a storm. But the real flavour of the morning comes together in the Market Burger – local bacon, Rosie's eggs, a bun from the Lyndoch Bakery and locally made chutney. And they are all the more tasty for the fact that they are sourced and cooked in the shed. The regulars issue a warning, however – have breakfast last, because the produce goes so fast that, if you don't, you'll miss out! Another good reason to wake up in the Barossa.

Vintner's Shed
Nuriootpa Road, Angaston
South Australia 5353
Tel (08) 8563 3603
Open Saturdays
7.30 am to 11.30 am (be early)

Barossa
Farmers'
Market

Chateau Tanunda

74 km
north-east
of Adelaide

with
Keith
Conlon

Just a few years ago Chateau Tanunda was a neglected and decrepit old sleeping giant near Tanunda. But now the giant is not only awake again, but it is also enjoying a whole new lifestyle.

The Chateau began in 1890 when hundreds of German grape-growers needed a big winery to take their vintages. British-born investors with export profits in mind imported cast-iron columns from Glasgow and oak from France and housed them in bluestone from Bethany and bricks baked on site. The result was an optimistic chateau that housed a million gallons of wine.

However, the corporate carry-on of the late twentieth century saw it languishing dangerously unloved and in need of a friend. That friend came along in 1998 in the form of John Geber who has spent five years and maybe five million dollars renovating what is an important part of Barossa heritage.

Chateau Tanunda is framed by giant palms

All set for a chateau banquet

Perched on the highest point of the Valley floor, it offers stunning views of the Barossa Valley and the Barossa Ranges beyond. The big palms on the front lawns frame the Chateau's twenty metre high tower and the magnificent building that can now store five million litres of wine.

Inside, a red gum tasting bench stretches into the cathedral of the barrel room and easily absorbs a visiting mini-bus group. They're welcome as long as they book for a structured tasting of the Chateau Tanunda whites and reds.

Upstairs, a lofty space that was slowly filling with pigeon droppings has been transformed into a spot for a slap-up do for several hundred, while in the Long Room, new windows offer fresh views of the vineyards through to Mengler's Hill. Add candles and fine cuisine and you're in for a European Chateau experience for a fraction of the price.

The Chateau also houses the Barossa Small Winemakers' Centre which shows off more than fifty labels from twenty small producers. A browse through the labels reveals the Barossa Germanic tradition holding strong – among them the Zander, Liebich, Rosenweig and Mader families, all operating their fifth-generation holdings. Chateau Tanunda is a true Barossa experience.

Basedow Road, Tanunda
South Australia 5352
Cellar doors open daily
10 am to 5 pm
Tel (08) 8563 3888
Email wine@chateautanunda.com
Web www.chateautanunda.com

Chateau
Tanunda

Doddridge Blacksmith Shop at Angaston

84 km
north-east
of Adelaide

with Lisa McAskill

Entering Doddridge Smithy Shop is like stepping back in time Photo by Colin Liebig

An old blacksmith shop in the main street of Angaston has been an important part of the town since 1847. It was built by Cornishman William Doddridge, one of the colony's early immigrants who originally landed on Kangaroo Island in 1837. A few years later he packed up his bellows and moved to the Barossa Valley.

The smithy business he set up here has certainly stood the test of time. It was passed from father to son for three generations of Doddridges. They never had far to go to work either because the family cottage is next door to the shop.

The last in line was Hardy Doddridge who took over the business as a sixteen-year-old at the turn of the last century. He worked the forge for 74 years and shod his last horse in 1981 at the age of 90. Hardy became a legend to the local Angaston kids and even today Mick Shemmeld says the smithy's shop is full of boyhood memories. 'Hardy would pick up a draught horse's hind leg and sometimes the horse would be a bit toey. Hardy would be flung up in the air and down on the floor but he wouldn't let the leg go,' Mick recounted. 'He would shoe that horse no matter what – he'd just hang on!'

Thankfully, the locals have rallied to reopen the old shop – complete with William Doddridge's original bellows. Mick and others like Don Harper continue to pound the anvil and sweat over the glowing coke to keep the smithy experience alive. The day we were there Don was making a cold chisel and in the process we learned a lesson or two

Hardy Doddridge shod his last horse at the age of 90

as the red hot metal began to lose its heat. 'The hot red colour is fading so if you try to shape it now it's liable to crack so we need to put it back in the fire and reheat it,' Don told us. 'That's where the saying, "strike while the iron is hot" comes from.'

A visit to the shop is certainly a step back in time. If you're lucky you might even get to don the leather apron and swing a hammer over the anvil like we did. Either way you can pick up a special memento like a metal gum leaf forged by earth, wind and fire at the Doddridge Blacksmith Shop in Angaston. It's open Saturday and Sunday afternoons or by appointment.

19 Murray St, Angaston
South Australia 5353
Open Saturday and Sunday
1 pm to 4 pm
Tel (08) 8564 2032
or (08) 8564 2349

A&H Doddridge
Blacksmith Shop

Food Barossa

84 km
north-east
of Adelaide

with
Lisa
McAskill

I n the tranquillity of the Barossa Valley behind Angaston an 1840s farmhouse has been transformed into a food factory. Farm Follies is where Jan Angas and others involved in a cooperative called Food Barossa are whipping up a storm. When we called in Jan was checking her range of chutneys made from fresh Barossa produce, while Rolf Egert sampled his latest batch of Kurianda olive oil, again sourced locally from trees growing wild in the gullies along the range.

The Barossa Valley is already known throughout the world for its wine and these people are determined to promote what they consider is a unique Australian regional cuisine developed over 150 years. Jan says modern Barossa cuisine draws its inspiration from the old German tradition of wasting nothing. The locals have experimented over the generations with different methods to preserve fresh herbs, fruit and other produce when they're plentiful so they can still be used when they're out of season.

The local food is flavoured with plenty of Barossa tradition

The locals work hard to preserve their Barossa-style cuisine

Food Barossa was launched in 2001 and now involves more than thirty local producers. The products include baked goods, smoked and fresh meats, condiments and sauces and even a wine label. Everything on sale has to be locally produced and meet stringent guidelines on methods and traditions unique to the local area.

And you don't have to venture far to sample the delights. Just pop into Murray Street, Angaston, to find Angaston Gourmet Food. For owner Aaron Penley, the emphasis is local and here you'll find the much-sought-after baguette known as the Barossa Beauty. It's a freshly baked roll full of traditional mettwurst, dill pickles and condiments. Like all of Food Barossa's products, it's a meal flavoured with years of Barossa valley tradition.

6/109 Murray Street, Tanunda
South Australia 5352
Tel (08) 8563 3603
Web www.foodbarossa.com

Food Barossa

PO Box 130, Angaston
South Australia 5353
Tel (08) 8564 8270

Farm Follies

Jacob's Creek Visitor Centre

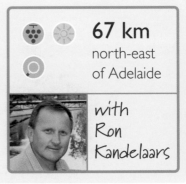

67 km north-east of Adelaide

with Ron Kandelaars

A small sign with a big reputation

When Bavarian settler Johann Gramp planted his first vines near an old cottage and cellar in 1847 little did he know that the grapes he was growing on the banks of Jacob's Creek would eventually release a flood of Australian wine to the world.

The sign marking Jacob's Creek is one of the most photographed spots in the Barossa Valley but it says much more about the history of the Valley and the marketing power of Australian wine in the twenty-first century.

The story of the tiny creek's dramatic impact on the wine scene is told at the new Jacob's Creek Visitor Centre where you can have a meal in the restaurant, browse through the cellar and, of course, taste the world's most popular Australian wine brand. It's an ultra modern building with views towards the Barossa Ranges and the red-gum-studded Jacob's Creek – the two features that have combined to produce the legend. For millions of years rain washed soil down from the ranges and deposited it on the flats along the river. Today it's those rich alluvial flats that produce high quality grapes that Orlando says are an important ingredient of its wine.

At the touch of a button, courtesy of the Centre's interpretive display, you get a lesson on how Johannes Menge, a self-taught mineralogist, helped persuade the German immigrants to settle in the Barossa Valley in 1842. Menge's reports also prompted the arrival of settlers like Johann Gramp and his wife, Eleanor. Johann produced one of the Barossa's first commercial vintages in 1850. Their original cottage has been restored and gives a wonderful glimpse of the beginning of what is now one of South Australia's biggest export industries.

The Jacob's Creek story and the Visitor Centre attracts wine lovers from all over the world and that's not surprising given that overseas is where most of the wine ends up. The day we were there we met John and Lyn from the UK. They described their visit as a 'bit of a pilgrimage'. They wanted to see where the wine they drink at home comes from. They planned to take a bottle or two back with them too. Brits travelling to the Barossa to buy Australian wine – surely it would have been all too much for old Johann Gramp and Johannes Menge.

By the way, Jacob's Creek was named after William Jacob, assistant surveyor to Colonel William Light. Jacob surveyed the area in 1839 and eventually

A modern centre in an historic landscape

built a winery here. The old Moorooroo cellar is now part of the Grant Burge Wine operation.

Barossa Valley,
between Rowland Flat and Tanunda
Tel (08) 8521 3000
Open daily 9.30 am to 5 pm
Free admission

Jacob's Creek
Visitor Centre

Lawley Farm Bed and Breakfast

74 km
north-east
of Adelaide

with
Lisa
McAskill

Lawley Farm is a great place to explore the valley's German past   Photo by Lesley Gregg

As you drive through the seemingly endless hectares of vines in the Barossa Valley, there are signs of the region's early European heritage everywhere. Get up close to many of the buildings and the classic Germanic construction speaks of a time when the early Silesian settlers made their way en masse to this part of South Australia.

August and Bertha Grocke arrived in Tanunda in 1851 and built what is now known as Lawley Farm. The original cottages and outbuildings have been converted into bed and breakfast accommodation by current owners Jack and Lesley Gregg, but the signs of August, Bertha and their four children's occupation of this little patch of the Barossa are everywhere. That includes a subterranean secret – a cellar – which, according to Jack, speaks volumes about the tenacity of the German settlers.

'We've been told the settlers used to dig a hole the size of the cellar they wanted, line the walls with ash and stone, fill it in again with sand, lay pavers on top of it and build their house. They'd wait some years for it to settle under its own weight and then dig it out again. The effort that went into building a cellar was just incredible.'

The Grocke cellar was used to store pickles, smoked meats and other foods needed to feed the family during the winter. It's the kind of self sufficiency that Jack, Lesley and their daughter Alexandra have also taken to heart as they and their guests go on the regular morning search for eggs.

The buildings have been beautifully restored | Dine in the historic cellar | Photos by Lesley Gregg

In the early days, the block would have been laid out in the German Hufendorf style with a long thin strip of land extending behind the house where Jack and Lesley now tend their vines.

Lesley explained how the houses were built along the road and the farmer's thin strip of land would extend at right angles to the road. 'Often the plot of land was only wide enough to allow the farmer to turn his horse and plough around.'

You can still make out the Hufendorf patterns from a hilltop lookout at nearby Bethany. Of course now the land is covered in vineyards.

Lawley Farm is the ideal base from which to explore and indulge in the Valley's early history. Across the road is the refurbished Silesian Barn, the work of local winemakers Grant and Helen Burge. You can walk to Rockford's Winery or go on a stroll around historic Bethany – a trip through the region's German past.

Krondorf Road, Tanunda
(near Rockford's Winery)
South Australia 5352
Tel (08) 8563 2141
Email lawleyfarm@ozemail.com.au

Lawley Farm

Williamstown — the Southern Gateway of the Barossa

48 km
north-east
of Adelaide

with
Keith
Conlon

ucked away on a creek that flows off the Barossa Range, Williamstown is certainly pretty enough to call itself the Scenic Southern Gateway of the Barossa. It's on the road between Chain of Ponds in the Adelaide Hills and the Barossa town of Lyndoch.

The day the *Postcards* team was there, we could see the pine trees of Mount Crawford Forest rising from the vines, and to the north the Mount Lofty Range meeting the rounded peaks of the Barossa Range. To the east lay the magnificent Forest Reserve with its long-standing commercial forest areas and big tracts of native bush.

The story of Williamstown is one of a timber town and it starts at the sprawling colonial-era hotel in the main street. Originally called the Victoria Creek Hotel, it served the labourers from the pastoral runs and the timber cutters and sawmillers who were turning giant gum trees into wharf and jetty pylons and railway sleepers. The pub was named after the stream running through the country of the Peramangk Aborigines who lived on the plentiful wildlife, permanent clear waters and sheltered in the giant red gums.

The Bakehouse Tavern used to be a butcher's shop and bakery   Foresters Hall   Photos by John Kammerman

And the town's name? Lewis Johnstone was moving a mob of horses through in 1857 when he stopped for a drink. He liked the place so much that he swapped his steeds for the hotel and surrounding land, subdivided a town around it, and named it after his son. 'William's town' was born.

The town's timber days are echoed on the hotel verandah where a long red gum trunk has been fashioned into a massive bench seat. In the old days, if you managed to lift it away from the wall and put it back, it was the publican's shout!

A stroll down the main street leads past the long standing general store to a quintessential country town Post Office. The Williamstonians have successfully fought to keep the peculiar spelling on its sign, a legacy of a long gone eccentric sign writer – 'Telegragh Office'.

Further along the street, some elements of the 1860s school are visible beside the new classrooms. Surely the pride of the town is the two-storey edifice on the main street. It began as a modest Council Chamber and by 1924 grew to become the Soldiers' Memorial Institute. It was the centre for all things social and recreational, including black and white silent movie nights.

Beside the road that winds down to Lyndoch in the Barossa Valley is the brightly painted Mechanics Institute – a tribute to the district's enthusiasm for self education during the nineteenth century. The tree cutters' fraternity, the Foresters Lodge, took it over in the 1920s, and these days it's one of several attractive B&B's round the town.

The creek glistening over a 1930s weir at the southern entrance to the town reminded us that this is still an important water and timber district. The South Para Reservoir is just a kilometre downstream.

Locals have fought hard to retain the sign on the Post Office　　Soldiers' Memorial Institute　　Photos by John Kammerman

There's an old stone bridge that was built to get the timber cutters and their horses across the swollen water torrent so that they could patronise the Cundy Brothers Blacksmith Shop that now dispenses baked goodies. The bridge leads to the Mount Crawford Forest of a million or so pines which is also a popular spot for campers and walkers. The Heysen and Mawson Trails snake along the forest and bush tracks through marvellous hills scenery.

Along the route out of Williamstown is an old sawmill turned cooperage. There used to be several mills in the region and the cutters and sawyers provided a livelihood for a number of quaint shops in town. Pick up an historical tour guide at the deli or bakery, and you'll easily find a dressed stone cottage that was once the local haberdashery. It's now a craft gallery.

Over the lane, there is a tiny building that was once home to an illegal betting shop while on the rise over the road there's another sandstone building from the 1850s that's been a butcher's shop and bakery, and now it welcomes travellers as the Old Bakehouse Tavern.

There are plenty of reasons why this is a place worthy of spending an afternoon or even a few days. And as they like to tell us, Williamstown is less than 50 kilometres and 50 minutes from Adelaide.

Between Kersbrook and Lyndoch
More information from the Barossa
Wine and Visitor Centre
Tanunda, South Australia 5352
Tel 1300 852 982

Williamstown —
Southern
Barossa
Gateway

Clare Valley and the Mid North

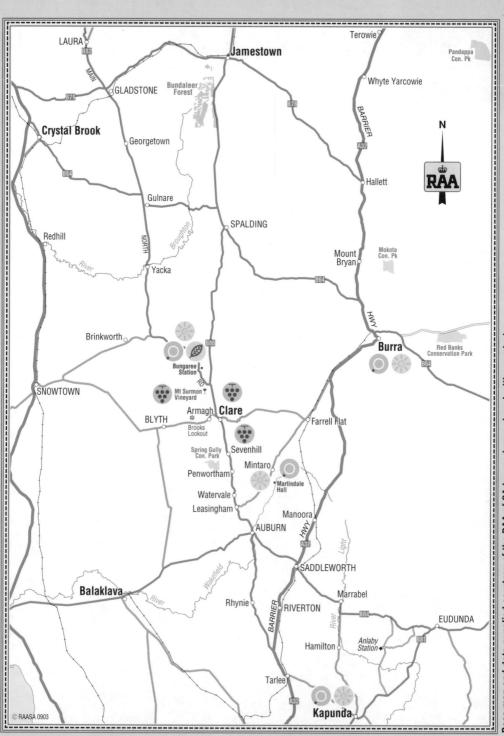

Food/Wine   Walking/Activity   History/Local Interest   Nature/Wildlife

N

RAA

LAURA
B82

Terowie

Pandappa
Con. Pk

Jamestown

Whyte Yarcowie

GLADSTONE
B79

Bundaleer
Forest

MAIN

BARRIER

A32

Crystal Brook

Georgetown

B64

Hallett

Gulnare

Redhill

NORTH

SPALDING

Mokota
Con. Pk

River

Broughton

Yacka

Mount
Bryan

B64

HWY

Brinkworth

B80

Burra

Red Banks
Conservation Park

B64

Bungaree
Station

SNOWTOWN

Mt Surmon
Vineyard

Armagh

Clare

Farrell Flat

BLYTH

Brooks
Lookout

Sevenhill

Spring Gully
Con. Park

Mintaro

Penwortham

Martindale
Hall

Watervale

Leasingham

Manoora

AUBURN

HWY

A32

Light

SADDLEWORTH

Balaklava

River

Rhynie

BARRIER

RIVERTON

Marrabel

B84

EUDUNDA

River

Wakefield

Anlaby
Station

B81

Hamilton

Tarlee

A32

Kapunda

© RAASA 0903

Base map and data supplied courtesy of the RAA of SA Inc. and reproduced with permission

Fields, Burra, Clare Valley

Views of rolling hills blanketed in immaculate vineyards, pockets of unspoiled bush, classic stone buildings and beautifully preserved heritage-listed towns greet you when touring through the Clare Valley and the Mid North.

This region is so close to Adelaide and yet so far away from the stresses of modern city life that it's easy to spend a day exploring the thirty-five or so cellar doors scattered throughout the five valleys that make up the grape-growing region. While the Clare Valley is considered the home of Australian riesling, its cool climate also produces world class cabernets and shiraz.

Before European settlement the area was good possum hunting country for the Ngadjuri people whose land stretched from Gawler to Orroroo. With the founding of the colony came the pastoralists and grape-growers. Stations were settled, homesteads and towns were built – many of which we can enjoy today. Make time to visit Bungaree and Anlaby Stations, or Martindale Hall. Classic towns like Clare, Auburn and Mintaro are ideal for a weekend stroll.

Then came the mining boom. After the chance discovery of copper by a sheep farmer, Kapunda became Australia's first mining town. More copper was found further north at Burra and thousands of miners from Cornwall and Wales descended on the Mid North in search of their fortune. By 1851 Burra's population had swelled to 5000 and its Monster Mine was producing the richest ore ever seen. Together, the two towns saved the flagging South Australian economy.

Today, it's as though time has stood still as you wander around the towns and drive through the countryside. It's a great way to blow off the woes of city life and, as they say, 'get closer' to a fascinating part of SA.

Tips from the Crew

• Trevor suggests stopping off at Farrell Flat, midway between Burra and Clare. It used to be a stopover point for the bullockies carting ore from Burra. There's an interpretive centre in the community gardens.

• Only 25 kilometres north of Clare visit Geralka Rural Farm and experience our pastoral and farming history. There are over 300 vintage farm machines, heritage buildings and farmyard animals.

• Lisa says a great place for morning or afternoon tea is the restored Riverton Railway Station. It was the site of Australia's first political assassination in 1921.

• Brenda suggests collecting a Burra Antique Trail brochure from the Burra Visitor Centre and following the trail around the township to visit the range of antique shops.

Top Attractions

Burra Passport

Collect a passport and key from the Burra Visitor Centre and visit the heritage sites and museums around the historic town of Burra. Some of the sites include Redruth Gaol, Unicorn Brewery Cellars and Miners Dugouts.

Riesling Trail

The Riesling Trail is a 27 kilometre pathway ideal for cyclists and walkers. Built on the old railway line between Clare and Auburn the trail meanders though some of the most varied and picturesque country in the Clare Valley.

Sevenhill Cellars

Established in 1851 by Jesuit priests Sevenhill Cellars is the oldest winery in the Clare Valley. Comprising St Aloysius Catholic Church and cemetery, and St Aloysius College and cellars, the complex is listed on South Australia's State Heritage Register.

Redbanks Conservation Park

Close to Burra the Redbanks Conservation Park is known for its mining history as well as being an important wildlife habitat. The park has deep meandering gorges, a disused gold mine and a number of dugouts.

Kapunda Heritage Trail

The Heritage Trail is a 10 kilometre trail through the old Kapunda mine area, past tunnels, open cuts and miners' cottages, highlighting the history and development of the town.

Samphire Discovery Trail

Just 9 kilometres from Two Wells is the Middle Beach Samphire Discovery Trail where you can stroll along the boardwalk and see mangrove forests, samphire flats and seagrass meadows.

Want More Information?

SA Visitor and Travel Centre
1300 655 276

Clare Valley Visitor Information Centre
1800 242 131

Clare Valley website
www.clarevalley.com.au

Burra Visitor Information Centre
(08) 8892 2154

Kapunda Visitor Information Centre
(08) 8566 2902

National Parks and Wildlife SA
(08) 8892 3025

RAA Touring (maps and guides)
(08) 8202 4600

SA Tourism Commission website
www.southaustralia.com

Postcards website
www.postcards-sa.com.au

I Didn't Know That

• Cattle king Sir Sidney Kidman lived in Kapunda for more than 40 years. His family home is now the main building of the Kapunda High School.

• In 1862 explorer John McDouall Stuart sent a telegram from Burra to the Governor of South Australia to advise him that he had successfully crossed Australia.

• Next time you play billiards it's likely you are playing on a slab of slate from Mintaro Slate Quarries. They've been exporting slate around the world for billiards tables since 1856.

• The Clare Valley's Riesling Trail is part of the famous Mawson Trail, a 900 kilometre bike trail from Adelaide to the Flinders Ranges.

• Morphett's Enginehouse museum is believed to be the only reconstructed Cornish Enginehouse outside Cornwell. It has three floors of information boards, display cases, models and explanatory videos.

Bungaree Station

146 km north of Adelaide

with Lisa McAskill

When you stand on a nearby hill and look down on historic Bungaree Station you look down on a virtual time capsule that tells a lot about South Australia's early pastoral history.

The view is dominated by the imposing old woolshed, Bungaree's first building. It was constructed in 1842 and was the hub of what was to become a village set on the outskirts of colonial civilisation.

In Bungaree's heyday, founder George Charles Hawker oversaw a team of fifty shearers working the shed. Now, come shearing season, a much smaller team of about ten tread the boards beneath the native pine rafters and shingled roof but the shed remains the backbone of the Bungaree legend.

It all began when George Hawker and his two brothers James and Charles overlanded two thousand sheep to a valley just north of Clare. On Christmas Day in 1841

Bungaree Homestead is now home to fourth and fifth generation Hawkers

Shearing time

Bungaree Station is a virtual time capsule

they sank a well and recorded that it had good drinkable water. They called their new home 'Bungurrie' – an Aboriginal word meaning 'my country' or 'place of deep water'. Over time 'Bungurrie' was anglicised to 'Bungaree'.

By the mid 1800s Bungaree had established itself as one of the great South Australian sheep runs and soon the Hawkers moved from a tent to a slab hut, then to a stone house. The magnificent homestead we see today grew over the years along with George and Bessie Hawker's family. They had sixteen children and as the family increased in size so did the homestead. Today it's still in the family, home for the fourth and fifth generations of Hawkers – George and Sal and their three children.

Pointing towards the imposing stone church Sal explained that her great grandfather-in-law, George, was a God-fearing man. The buggy ride into Clare for Sunday Service was a three-hour round trip so he used to conduct his own services in the woolshed. As his sheep flock grew so did his staff and when his 'woolshed congregation' reached 100 he decided it was time to build a proper church.

The Church of England chapel called St Michael's was completed in 1864. It was the only building on the estate to be designed by an architect – Edward Hamilton, who just happened to be George's brother-in-law. Despite its obvious charm, which includes hand-painted stained-glass

A great country experience

Photo by Jeff Clayfield

The station store has been restored | The woolshed was the first building at Bungaree Photo by Jeff Clayfield

windows, St Michael's didn't prove to be as popular as the non-denominational wood-shed. Not all the staff were Anglican so the congregation almost halved. Regular services are still held at St Michael's and it's a popular wedding venue too.

Sal showed us another piece of Bungaree's history – the old stallion stable. Originally built to pamper the station's valued stallion and keep him away from the mares, it has undergone a thorough renovation and is now a much-sought-after honeymoon suite. It's one of a range of accommodation options that includes the Manager's House, Shearer's Quarters and Heritage Cottages. Bungaree Station offers a kids-friendly country experience and gives a great insight into nineteenth-century pastoral history.

PO Box 231, Clare
South Australia 5453
Tel (08) 8842 2677
Email info@bungareestation.com.au
Web www.bungareestation.com.au
Tours by arrangement

Bungaree
Station

Gourmet Delights in the Clare Valley

106 km north of Adelaide

with Ron Kandelaars

Being only a little over an hour from Adelaide, Clare Valley is the perfect place to unwind. It's actually made up of five valleys and takes in the town of Clare and six smaller villages including Auburn and Mintaro. There are more than 30 cellar doors and with so many picture postcard settings it's not hard to see why it attracts nearly a quarter of a million visitors every year.

One of the best times to visit is during the annual Gourmet Weekend which is held each May. More than twenty wineries team up with local and Adelaide restaurants to offer food, wine and music combinations for every taste.

One of them is Eldredge Vineyard Restaurant at Sevenhill. Winemaker Leigh Eldredge has transformed a 1920s dairy farm into a winery delight. 'There was a little dairy here when we bought it in 1993. No one had lived here for about fifteen years and

Eldredge Vineyard Restaurant is a popular place during the gourmet weekend   Photo by Charles Cannon Design

the cows and sheep had been through it,' explained Leigh.

The old dairy and cottage is now a winery and restaurant and it's the locals and visitors who do the grazing on the balcony overlooking the farm dam. The emphasis is on local wine and produce and Chef Phil Scalres brings new meaning to the culinary concept of 'surf and turf' – his version is 'lamb and dam'. The lamb is from the saltbush plains near Burra, and the yabbies from the dam below. After the *Postcards* team's taste-

Make time for some wine tasting

test I can assure you it's a dish worth trying and it's just one of the sensations on offer at the Eldredge Vineyard Restaurant on Spring Gully Road.

Spring Gully Road, Sevenhill
South Australia
Tel (08) 8842 3086
Tastings daily 11 am to 5 pm
Lunch Thursday to Sunday
Weekend bookings essential

Eldredge
Vineyard and
Restaurant

Third weekend of May
Contact Clare Valley
Winemakers' Association
Tel (08) 8843 0222
Email cvwi@capri.net.au

Clare
Gourmet
Weekend

Kapunda the Copper Town

106 km
north-east
of Adelaide

with Keith Conlon

The town of Kapunda moves at an easy pace these days but if you look carefully, an old mine chimney stack and an array of fine buildings reveal the wealth that once flowed down its streets. In 1838 squatters Francis Dutton and his neighbour Captain Charles Bagot stumbled across some copper outcrops while searching for stray sheep.

They kept their find secret for two years while they had it properly analysed overseas. It soon became apparent they were sitting on a copper lode of staggering potential – the highest grade of ore found anywhere in the world. They bought the land, announced their find and built the copper mining town of Kapunda.

By 1844 the first of thousands of Cornish miners had arrived. They were followed by the Welsh smelters, then the Irish labourers and the German farmers. All of this happened at a time when the young colony of South Australia was at a point of economic collapse so the discovery helped save South Australia from bankruptcy.

Initially, the early Cornish miners formed groups and would tender for an area of exposed ore body and were paid according to its value. There was little supervision and over time a series of haphazard burrows developed. Later underground mining gave way to open cut, but by 1879 the mine was closed. Today you can still make sense of the maze of shafts and mine workings via the well marked interpretative trail. It includes a lookout over the giant open cut.

Dutton and Bagot became fabulously wealthy and the town boomed. Much of that wealth is now reflected in Kapunda's wonderful architectural heritage like a Romanesque-type building in Hill Street which was constructed as a Baptist Church in 1866. It now houses the Kapunda Museum.

The Museum is considered one of the best folk museums in South Australia. It highlights how life changed with the influx of mineral wealth and later how the agricultural boom transformed rural life. There's a flying fox that was used to send the money from the counter to the cashier in the old Farmer's Cooperative Store; a display of the Mellor Crop Stripper that was built there; an audio video display about the local Hawke Foundry; and the presses from the Kapunda *Northern Star*, one of the first country newspapers in South Australia.

You can also pick up a Heritage Trail brochure from the Visitor Information Centre up the road from the Museum. Use it to follow Tourist Drive No. 17 to discover a range of other heritage-listed buildings.

11 Hill Street, Kapunda
South Australia 5373
Tel (08) 8566 2286
Open daily 1 pm to 4 pm
between September and May
Open 1 pm to 4 pm weekends,
school holidays and public holidays
from June to August
Other times by appointment
Town tours also available

Kapunda
Museum

51 Main Street, Kapunda
South Australia 5373
Tel (08) 8566 2902
Open Monday to Friday
10 am to 4 pm,
weekends 10 am to 4 pm

Kapunda Visitor
Information
Centre

Left: the old Baptist church is now the museum; centre: the old mine site on the edge of town; and right: Map the Miner greets visitors to Kapunda

Photos by Jeff Clayfield

Martindale Hall — a Living Museum

120 km
north of
Adelaide

with
Lisa
McAskill

Martindale Hall is the grand old dame of the mid north. The nineteenth-century Georgian mansion sits on a rise just outside Mintaro and is one of the Clare Valley's most recognisable icons.

Many have fallen under her spell including film maker Peter Weir who, in 1975, used it as the setting for the girls' boarding school in his film *Picnic at Hanging Rock*. The film not only launched his career and revived Australia's film industry, it also indirectly saved Martindale Hall. According to Martindale's current lessee, John Maguire, the film is still the main reason many people visit.

When you do you enter another world – one of fabulous wealth at a time when a 21-year-old sheep farmer named Edmund Bowman was determined to be noticed. He began building the house in 1879 and had 60 workers camping in tents for the two years it took to build.

One of the Clare Valley's most recognised buildings

The Bowmans made their money as pastoralists but Edmund was eventually forced to sell up following the devastating 1885 drought. In 1891 William Tenant Mortlock purchased the property. The Mortlocks were merchants with banking interests in England and fabulous property holdings around the state which allowed them to ride out the bad times and indulge themselves during the good times.

And that's exactly what they did – William's son, J.T. Mortlock, is responsible for much of Martindale's impressive collection. Enter his smoking room and you find it preserved exactly as it was on the day he died in 1950. It's a time-capsule full of the trophies and mementos of a man who spent years travelling through darkest Africa and the jungles of Sri Lanka. From 400-year-old ceremonial Samurai suits to Persian swords and spears from New Guinea – these remarkable artefacts are all on display in this gentleman's retreat.

The grand foyer and entrance hall of the mansion are magnificent. Overhead is a stunning replica of the original gasolier that illuminated the many grand balls and gatherings held in the hall in the early years.

It's one of the many features that make Martindale Hall one of the Australia's most impressive colonial mansions. But ask John Maguire and he'll tell you that what makes Martindale Hall truly unique is its accessibility. 'You can use and enjoy it … become Lord or Lady of the manor for a day.'

A range of bed and breakfast and dinner options are available and it's open to the public. On entry you get a brochure on the history of the house and there's a story about each room and its contents. Watch out also for the 'Incident at Martindale' nights when guests have to solve a crime over a four-course silver service dinner.

Open Monday to Friday
11 am to 4 pm,
Saturday and Sunday
Noon to 4 pm
Entry fee
(08) 8843 9088
Email marthall@chariot.net.au

Martindale Hall
via Mintaro

Mintaro Maze

☀ **130 km**
north of
Adelaide

with
Lisa
McAskill

The maze is a living design Photo by Sharon Morris

'Up periscope' Photo by Sharon Morris

Here's one for the kids on your next visit to Mintaro. Whether they are four or four-teen, they'll get a kick out of another man's folly that is the Mintaro Maze. The locals dubbed Mick Morris 'Mad Mick' years ago when he began planting rows and rows of conifers on his block on Jacka Road. A man of mystery, Mick never told anyone at the local pub what he was planning. Now, eight years and more than 800 Castewallan Gold Conifers later, the maze is a popular local attraction.

The day *Postcards* visited, Mick's love of a good puzzle had the kids from the nearby

Mintaro Farrell Flat Primary School in a spin as they tried to find their way out. I soon learned to trust my own instincts and not those of Millie, the resident Jack Russell. She's small enough to duck under or through the rows of trees to freedom. With some help from the kids, I soon figured out that the best thing to do is make your way to the centre of the maze and work your way out from there. But that's easier said than done.

Mick and his wife, Sharon, originally had visions of a maze to rival Hampton Court in England but they opted for their own intricate design – something that would fit on their country block.

Along the way it's been quite a talking point, especially on the day a passing farmer stopped for a brief chat. He got out of his car and asked Mick what he was planting. Mick yelled back that he was planting a maze. The farmer looked puzzled, threw his hands in the air and said, 'That's not how you plant maize!' and drove off.

That sort of thing doesn't happen now. Visitors take up the challenge of beating the intricate living design or playing a game of chess or noughts and crosses with giant pieces carved from the nearby Mintaro Slate Quarry. There's also a gift shop and a display of Christmas lights in December. So head to Mintaro for an 'amazing' experience.

Anyone for chess? Giant chess that is!
Photo by Sharon Morris

Jacka Road, Mintaro
South Australia 5415
Open Thurs to Monday
10 am to 4 pm (Closed February)
Tel (08) 8843 9012

Mintaro
Maze Garden

Mongolata Gold Mine at Burra

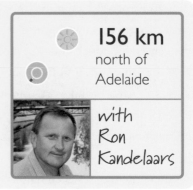

156 km
north of
Adelaide

with
Ron
Kandelaars

B urra is well known as one of Australia's historic copper mining towns. The 'Monster Mine' followed the discovery of copper by two shepherds in 1845. By the 1850s the operation was the richest copper mine in the world.

But copper wasn't the only thing to lure the hopeful miners – there was also gold to be found. And when you browse through the Mongolata Gold Gift Shop in Burra's Commercial Street it's not hard to see what captivated the shop's owner, Kevin Wallis, as a young lad. The place is crammed with colourful rocks, from malachite and fluorite to some of the purest gold found anywhere. The day we called in Wally, as he's known

Llife was tough for the miners – some lived on rations alone

to his mates, was proudly showing off a gold nugget that was one hundred per cent pure. 'It's perfect. You can't get any better than that,' he said with a grin.

That's why you'll often find Wally at his 'other' office – the working Mongolata Gold Mine, 23 kilometres east of town. We joined him on one of his regular tours and after fitting our hard hats he took us into the main drive where you get a real sense that you are entering another world full of the promise of gold. Wally explained what drives him. 'It's a real adrenalin buzz when you strike gold. You keep it for a while and eventually sell it and keep looking for more. When you find another piece you get that buzz again. It's like your first piece. That's what gets you hooked.'

Monster Mine, Burra

Mongolata wouldn't be a real goldfield without a few tales of gold fever and the strange things that people have done in search of their fortune. Wally tells the story about Teddy Bywaters who first discovered gold. Another bloke, Harry Byles, got him drunk in the local pub and found out the location. Byles then staked the claim and beat Teddy to the gold.

The lure of striking it rich keeps Wally coming back

It's said it drove Teddy crazy and after that he'd wander around in the bush at Mongolata trying to throw others off the scent by claiming his real find was elsewhere in the scrub. No one believed him and soon Harry Byles had some nuggets on display in a shop window in Burra and the rush was on.

That was in 1930 and by 1933 the Premier had opened the new battery which is now part of Wally's Tour. But the price of gold collapsed during the Depression and many of the miners stayed on for rations alone. Wally takes us to some ruins of an old boarding house that shows how tough life must have been. 'It was started by Bill Carpenter in 1933. There used to be a big dining room that would seat fifty blokes at a time. They'd pay fifteen shillings a week for a daily three-course meal,' Wally explained. 'So the miners who were earning some money could at least eat well. The rest of the blokes lived on rations or rabbits or whatever they could get their hands on.'

Many of the blokes left the goldfield at the outbreak of World War II and the mine finally closed in 1954. Now Wally runs the entire operation by himself and he still has hopes that the old mine vault will one day burst at the seams again as it was in 1935 when the great Mongolata Gold Heist saw two wheat bags crammed with gold stolen.

'The detectives came up from Adelaide and questioned all the miners. The mine manager was above reproach so he wasn't questioned.' But we can't reveal what happened in the end – you'll have to join one of Wally's mine tours to find out.

Mongolata Gold
3 Commercial Street, Burra
South Australia 5417
Tel (08) 8892 2233
Tour bookings essential

Mongolata
Gold Mine

Mount Surmon Winery and Gallery

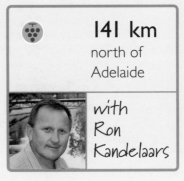

141 km north of Adelaide

with Ron Kandelaars

Perched on tiny Mount Surmon

The Clare Valley has long been a magnet for artists intent on capturing the changing seasons and colours of this world-renowned wine growing region. And if you head just north of Clare to Mount Surmon you'll come across the latest addition to the Valley's unique blend of art and wine.

The day we dropped in Adelaide artist John Illsley had commandeered a special spot in the car park. For fifty years he has managed to combine his two passions: interpreting South Australia's distinctive landscapes in watercolours, and travelling the state's many back roads as a stock agent and photographer.

He likes the mid north in particular. 'I see a lot of beauty and I like to capture the harshness of the vivid reds, ochres and oranges.' You can see the result of his labours on the walls of Scarlatties Gallery, part of the Mount Surmon Winery. The exhibits are changed regularly but the paintings of classic Mid North scenes of woolsheds, barns and cottages whet the appetite for anyone setting off north of Clare. As John points out, the scenes reflect how hard it must have been for the people who opened up the country.

Stand on top of Mount Surmon and you'll see many such pioneering scenes including wonderful views towards the Flinders Ranges, but enter the winery, gallery

Jeni and Burt Surmon

and retreat and you find the emphasis is on minimalist architecture and bold and modern colours.

Burt and Jeni Surmon told us they fell in love with the Clare Valley during a weekend escape from a restoration project in Adelaide. 'The penny suddenly dropped. This is where we needed to spend the rest of our lives.'

The colours they used in their buildings reflect the vibrant gold of the local canola crops and the vines in autumn. There's also a lot of purple which harks back to the days when they pulled out Salvation Jane and planted rows of shiraz and cabernet merlot in their vineyard.

They bought the land ten years ago when it was run-down farming land divided by a rusty barbed-wire fence. They lived in a galvanised iron shed while their house was built and spent three years planting their first vines. 'There's a certain romance attached to a vineyard but let me tell you, when you're actually hoeing out the weeds it's a lot of hard yakka.'

So from hard yakka to the fulfilment of a dream, Burt and Jeni's blend of wine, art and stunning views is a now a reality. Scarlatties is the cellar door and gallery and tucked away underneath is The Retreat, a suite for two. Mount Surmon Vineyard is open on Fridays and weekends. It's about six kilometres north of Clare on the road to Jamestown. Just look for the sign.

Basham Road (off Stradbrooke),
North Clare
South Australia 5453
Tel (08) 8842 1250
Email mtsurmon@rbe.net.au

Mount Surmon
Vineyard,
Gallery and
Retreat

Fleurieu Peninsula

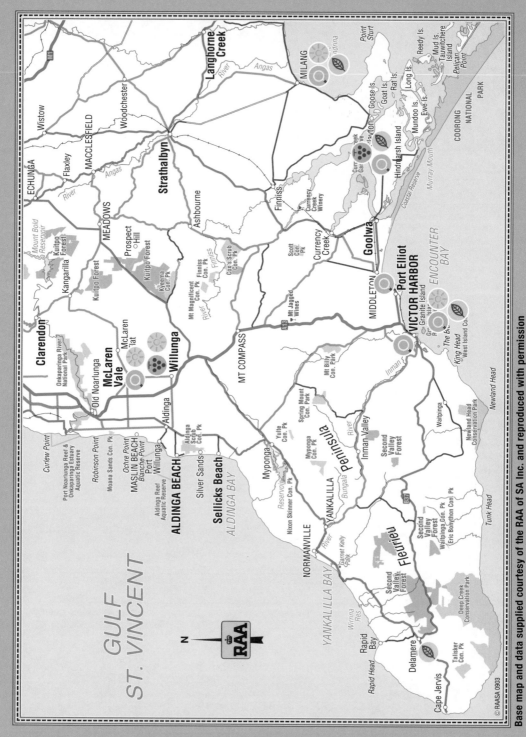

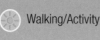

Food/Wine   Walking/Activity   History/Local Interest   Nature/Wildlife

Coastline, Sellicks Beach

The Fleurieu Peninsula is Adelaide's playground – a favourite destination for thousands of Adelaide families who make the pilgrimage every summer to the usually quiet towns along the coast. But there's more to the Fleurieu than fun summer holidays. It's a year-round destination offering an endless array of activities.

A day trip from Adelaide can take in some incredibly varied landscape. You can fast-track via the Southern Expressway to the vine-covered hills of McLaren Vale or take the scenic route via Clarendon and Kangarilla. Stick to the coast to marvel at the coloured cliffs of Port Willunga and Aldinga Bay and, further south, the sheer cliffs that drop into the ocean at Yankalilla Bay. Or, take the back way through the Mount Lofty Ranges and you'll dissect the undulating plains before arriving at sleepy hollows like Milang on the banks of giant Lake Alexandrina.

There are 30 national parks on the peninsula and one of the most rugged is Deep Creek. This park is at the south-east end of the Fleurieu and here you'll find untouched bushland and lonely views across Backstairs Passage to Kangaroo Island.

The unofficial capital of the Fleurieu is Victor Harbor – just the place to grab a feed of fish 'n' chips or an ice-cream before venturing across the causeway to Granite Island or climbing aboard a boat for a spot of whale-watching.

Goolwa is Australia's only registered inland port and the Signal Point River Murray Interpretive Centre revives the bustling days of the riverboat era. Goolwa is also the place from which to explore the world famous Coorong National Park. Camp Coorong, near Meningie, is a great place to learn about the connection the traditional owners, the Kaurna and Ngarrindjeri people, have to the land.

It is certainly worth lingering a while on the Fleurieu Peninsula.

Tips from the Crew

• Jeff says dawn and dusk are the best times to take photos on Granite Island because the rocks almost come alive with colour.

• Trevor says the kids will enjoy a visit to the huge adventure playground at Port Noarlunga. There is so much play equipment it'll be hard to tear them away.

• Ron says you don't need to stay at home just because it's raining. There are heaps of museums and antique stores throughout the Fleurieu to keep you occupied.

• The Cockle Train between Victor Harbor and Goolwa is a 'must do' part of your Fleurieu experience. Lisa points out that it is only steam-powered on some Sundays and during school holidays. At other times it's a rail car but still great fun.

Top Attractions

The Murray Mouth

See the Murray Mouth from Sugars Beach on Hindmarsh Island and learn about the ongoing dredging program to keep the mouth open.

Hindmarsh Island Bridge

Walk to the middle of the Hindmarsh Island Bridge for great views of Goolwa and the surrounding area.

Mount Compass Produce Trail.

Explore the Mount Compass Produce and Tourist Trail and pick up lots of interesting home-grown food and wine. You'll find maps at the tourist centre.

Port Elliot

Learn about Port Elliot's maritime history and shipwrecks at Freeman Nob, a vantage point with unparalleled views along the Encounter Bay coast.

Clayton Wetlands

Discover the wetlands walking trail and boardwalk at Clayton, a Ramsar area of international significance for migratory birds.

Encounter Bikeway

Follow the Encounter Bikeway along the coast between Goolwa and Victor Harbor. Pick up a brochure from the tourist centres.

Whale Watching

See the southern right whales from Basham's Beach at Middleton. The whale season usually runs from June to September.

Bird Watching

Explore the Snipe Sanctuary on the Milang foreshore. It is the seasonal home of Latham's snipe, small birds that migrate each year from Japan.

Cockle Train

Travel from Goolwa to Victor Harbor on SteamRanger's famous Cockle Train.

Want More Information?

SA Visitor and Travel Centre
1300 655 276

Fleurieu Peninsula website
www.fleurieupeninsula.com.au

McLaren Vale and Fleurieu Visitor Centre
(08) 8323 9944

Victor Harbor Information Centre
(08) 8552 5738

Goolwa Information Centre
(08) 8555 1144

National Parks and Wildlife SA
(08) 8552 3677

RAA Touring (maps and guides)
(08) 8202 4600

SA Tourism Commission website
www.southaustralia.com.au

***Postcards* website**
www.postcards-sa.com.au

I Didn't Know That

• The Heysen Trail starts on the tip of Fleurieu Peninsula at Cape Jervis then winds along 1500 kilometres of marked trail all the way to the Flinders Ranges.

• The Aldinga Scrub Conservation Park is home to more than 166 different bird species, 18 species of butterflies and 540 species of other insects.

• There are 8 tapered roller bearings beneath each of Granite Island's horse-drawn trams. It takes a pull of about 50 kilograms to move a loaded tram.

• The feature film *Heaven's Burning* starring Russell Crowe was filmed at Rapid Bay in 1997. Scenes were also filmed in Adelaide, Dry Creek and near Port Wakefield.

• The Fleurieu Peninsula was named after Charles-Pierre Claret de Fleurieu, the navigator who drew up the orders for the Baudin expedition to Southern Australia. We adopted the name in 1911 after a visit to SA by the Count's grand nephew.

Alexandrina Cheese Company at Mount Compass

67 km south of Adelaide

with Ron Kandelaars

For a certain herd of well-fed Jersey cows, their life on the picturesque Fleurieu Peninsula is pretty good. They represent the culmination of a dream for a family whose members have come from different parts of the globe to set up a dairy farm with a difference – the Alexandrina Cheese Company.

When you visit the cheesery midway between Mount Compass and Victor Harbor there's a fair chance one or more members of the families that run the place will be on hand to help with a tasting.

The secret of success Photo by Krystyna McCaul

It all began with George and Cathe Manowski. George emigrated from war-torn Poland in 1949 and bought the farm soon after marrying Cathe. These days, their daughter Krystyna and her husband, Dan McCaul, take care of the milking and that's when the cheese-making secrets begin to come to the fore.

Dan's father, Kevin, is the master cheesemaker, a trade he learned from his Irish father. His techniques have certainly been well tried and tested over the years and that's what makes the cheeses so different. We watched as Dan carried out the morning ritual of turning the cheddar in an open vat. 'The use of open vats is just one of the more traditional techniques we use. It's how Dad was taught and his father before him. It really makes a difference.'

So too does the use of homemade starters and animal based rennet which are made on site and not bought in bulk. The Alexandrina Cheese team sticks as closely as

Another batch maturing to perfection

Photo by Krystyna McCaul

possible to the traditional methods that have served them well for more than 50 years.

After the cream has been separated, the starter culture and rennet is added. It's then up to the stirring blades and nature to work their magic. After half an hour or so the mixture separates into curds and whey and Kevin gives the all clear to begin cutting what will become another batch of English Cheddar.

Meanwhile, batches of Dutch Edam and Gouda were being salted and dipped in brine before being set aside to mature. The Alexandrina Cheese Company is the only producer of Edam and Gouda in South Australia so they're really worth trying. While we enjoyed our sample in the tasting room the marketing manager, Becky, who's Dan and Krystyna's daughter, joked about how their cheeses begin with a vat of milk, some rennet and a dash of culture – some Irish and some Polish!

The Alexandrina Cheese Company is on Sneyd Road at Mount Jagged. Look for the turn-off as you pass Mount Compass on the way to Victor Harbor. It's number 24 on the Produce Trail and is open weekends and public holidays. Oh, and while you're there, try their double cream – it's heaven!

Sneyd Road, Mount Jagged
South Australia
Farm gate shop open Saturday,
Sunday and public holidays
10 am to 4.30 pm
Tel (08) 8554 9666
Email alexandrinacc@ozemail.com.au

Alexandrina
Cheese
Company

Dog Dragon at Port Elliot

82 km south of Adelaide

with Lisa McAskill

Behind a classy little shop-front on Port Elliot's main street there's a treasure trove of furniture and artefacts collected during one man's love affair with our northern neighbour – Indonesia.

As a young surfer John Beach first visited Indonesia 20 years ago in search of the perfect wave but became increasingly fascinated with the country's many and varied islands, the people and their way of life. So much so that he and his wife, Annie, now run an importing business called Dog Dragon.

The shop contains some amazing pieces. The day I was there John was working on an old teak lesong – a huge wooden mortar from Java, used to grind rice. John reckoned it had seen plenty of work because a hole had been ground right through its bottom. Levelled off and covered with a sheet of plate glass it's now a unique coffee table.

John still heads north four or five times a year and always comes back with

The Indonesian influence is strong at Dog Dragon

Photo by Annie Beach

There's a treasure trove behind the shop front Photos by Annie Beach

a collection of fascinating pieces, some that are very traditional but which also catch the eye of the more adventurous interior designers. John likes to describe the collection as being a bit like 'teak tupperware' – there's a piece for almost every use.

The Dog Dragon showroom is worth a visit any time – even if it's only to breathe the wonderful aroma of teak.

55 North Terrace, Port Elliot
South Australia 5212
Tel (08) 8554 2388
Open Friday to Saturday
10 am to 5 pm,
Sunday Noon to 5 pm,
and other days during school holidays

Dog
Dragon

The Encounter Centre at Victor Harbor

83 km south of Adelaide

with Lisa McAskill

L ooking for something a little different on your trip through the Fleurieu? We found just the thing on the outskirts of Victor Harbor – The Encounter Centre. One look at the faces of the people who work here and you can see they love what they do.

The Encounter Centre is best known as a wooden toy factory and plant nursery and it relies on volunteers to help run the activities for people with special needs. The day we were there Craig Walker, who lost his sight as a kid, was painstakingly sanding a wooden truck. He's a qualified masseur and he told us that he's been coming here for more than seven years so the Centre has been a big part of his life.

The money earned from the sale of the toys and plants is poured back into the Centre. The range of products is enormous – wooden tug-boats, planes, trains, dolls houses and rocking horses and even furniture. They also take orders. The nursery is a new initiative and specialises in plants potted up in unusual containers, some of which are made in the Centre. They make wonderful gifts.

Putting the finishing touches to some wooden toys

The plant nursery is new

The Encounter Centre is a real success story – a few years ago they ran a marketing campaign to promote their products but they had to withdraw the campaign because they couldn't keep up with the demand!

But it's not just people with special needs who benefit. There are plenty of able-bodied people who get a chance to do something new. People like Danny Moerland, a former architect, and Ian Gillespie, a former railway worker. They were at a bit of a loss about how to fill in their time after they retired so they began coming here and now swap yarns and wood-working techniques.

The range of toys and plants is fantastic as is the enthusiasm that keeps the place running. Everyone ultimately wins – the children who take home the toys, the volunteers who make them and those who profit from the sales.

The Encounter Centre is on the Armstrong Road at Victor Harbor. Just follow the turn-off at Urimbirra Wildlife Park on the Adelaide to Victor Road.

Armstrong Road (Ring Road),
Victor Harbor,
South Australia 5211
Tel (08) 8552 2995
Open Monday to Friday
9 am to 4 pm
Web www.encountercentre.com.au

The
Encounter
Centre

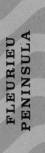

FLEURIEU PENINSULA

Granite Island

☀ **83 km** south of Adelaide

with Keith Conlon

A Granite Island welcome

Photo by Matthew Glastonbury

The famous horse tram has been trundling holiday makers across the causeway to Granite Island at Victor Harbor for about 110 years, but lately passengers are pleasantly surprised at the many changes on the island – especially the penguins who call it home.

As you come off the causeway you are greeted by a couple of statements that emphasise this is a special place. Some big polished granite boulders have the island's Aboriginal name, Kaiki, carved on them, and a bronze sculpture of penguins gives a taste of what's to come.

There are a number of raised wooden walkways around this section of the Granite Island Nature Park because, as our guide Amy Pysden pointed out, about 1800 Little Penguins call the island home. 'By keeping the pathway off the ground the penguins can pass underneath on their daily walks between the ocean and their burrows.'

The path that circumnavigates the island is the Kaiki Trail. It's 1.5 kilometres long and it takes about 40 minutes to walk around. There are plenty of seats and lookouts along the way. The trail is punctuated with interpretive signs, one of which graphically depicts the molten up-swelling of base rock that originally formed the island and the effects of the southern ocean swells on the solid granite.

Kaiki means 'reed spear' in the language of the Ngarrindjeri nation, and their Dreaming tells how the legendary warrior Ngurunderi threw his spear into the sea and created the island. Amy and the other tour guides also read an approved story about Umbrella Rock on the south-west side of the island. It's one of the island's most

photographed features and the story tells of Ngurunderi throwing another spear and his club, creating Wright Island and the Bluff to the west.

The South Australian Company made its mark in the first months of the colony by starting a whaling station at the foot of the Bluff. But a privateer whaling master, Captain Blenkinsop, cheekily set up his operation on Granite Island near the first horse tram bend. Whenever a Southern Right Whale was sighted, the Southern Ocean side of the island was the scene of a dangerous competition between the whaling crews. Thankfully neither station was very successful.

As the region developed Victor became an important port. In the 1870s the causeway was built to take wool and grain to the island where smaller boats transferred it to the tall ships anchored in the bay. In 1882 the government sank a fortune into the screwpile jetty which meant the towering clipper ships could be loaded directly for their London run.

The 300 metre granite breakwater protruding east into Encounter Bay was built to protect the anchorage from ocean breakers. On our Granite Island Discovery Tour, Amy explained what a mammoth task it was. Four men died in the process of chiselling and blasting 192,000 tonnes of rock, rolling it on an extended railway and dropping it into the sea.

The quarry between the bistro and the breakwater has undergone a complete transformation. There's another raised boardwalk and some new miniature sand

The famous horse tram across the causeway

Photo by Matthew Glastonbury

dunes that allow the penguins free passage between the breakwater and their burrows among the granite boulders under the cliff.

Nightly two-hour-long penguin tours now include this boardwalk and close-up penguin traffic is guaranteed thanks to the 60 burrows installed by volunteers.

During the day, your first port of call should be to the information centre housed in the contemporary building perched above the breakwater. It's the place to go to find out about penguin tours, the floating Oceanarium (reached via a short boat trip), whale and island cruises, and guided tours for schools, groups and individuals. It's run by the lessees of the island, the Granite Island Nature Park Company, who work closely with the state's National Parks and Wildlife Service and Ngarrindjeri elders.

It also includes a bistro which overlooks the bay where seals and dolphins beckon. Or you can do what I still love – indulge in a simple, old fashioned pleasure – licking an ice cream from the kiosk and watching the waves break into sprays of white foam on the giant boulders of Granite Island.

Victor Harbor
South Australia 5211
Tel (08) 8552 7555
Email info@graniteisland.com.au
Web www.graniteisland.com.au
Penguin tours at dusk –
bookings essential

Granite Island
Nature Park

POSTCARDS·PO

Above: A great place to unwind

Photo by Matthew Glastonbury

Milang — Historic Port on the Lake

73 km
south-east
of Adelaide

with
Keith
Conlon

The historic port of Milang sits on a limestone rise overlooking one of Australia's largest inland lakes, Lake Alexandrina. Two cultures came together to form the names – Lake Alexandrina was named after the British princess who would soon become Queen Victoria, while a tribe of the Ngarrindjeri Aboriginal nation called the area 'a place of sorcery', Milangk.

These days Milang is best known as the town with the collection of quaint brightly hued shacks that make up an exclusive community right on the shore of the lapping lake. The miniature holiday houses crowded along the bank have become a Milang landmark complete with their own flimsy private jetties.

The colourful shacks are a Milang feature

But there's much more to Milang than the shacks – the town has a rich river trade history. It began in 1830 when Captain Sturt rowed his whale boat across the lake on his epic exploratory journey (during which he named Lake Alexandrina). The overlanders followed

The Pier Hotel overlooks Lake Alexandrina Photo by Alex Stone

and the country was soon opened up. Goolwa was established downstream and by the 1850s the idea of a port at Milang was considered a very good idea, especially for the commercial operators of Strathalbyn, who anticipated the opening up of the Murray-Darling Basin.

In 1857 an Adelaide newspaper reported that 'Milang is becoming a very bustling little port and will shortly grow into a place of importance'. And it did. The official signs of prosperity and culture were soon in place including two inns, a steam mill, a store, chapel, timber yard and a jetty. The best way to explore the history today is to grab a copy of Milang's new heritage map which pinpoints substantial buildings like the institute, post office and old police station.

At the end of today's jetty, which is half its original length since the Great Flood of 1956, there's another of Milang's claims to fame – a brightly painted hand crane which is the oldest in South Australia. It was erected for cargo handling in 1859, in the very early days of the port.

There was once much banging and sawing by the shore of the lake. Frank Potts, the legendary founder of the 1850 Bleasdale Winery at nearby Langhorne Creek, built several paddlesteamers here. The Church of England's floating chapel, the mission boat *Etona*, was locally built (it now resides at Echuca), and the ambitious Landseer Drydock was originally built here before being floated upstream to Mannum. The grand old lady of the Murray, PS *Marion*, also began life as a Milang-built barge in 1877.

The old railway line runs along the floodbank in front of the town. It began a little after the heady days of the paddlesteamer era, but it served the town well with the last passenger train departing in 1970. The picturesque weatherboard station is now a railway museum and also serves tea and scones on weekends and holidays.

It is also the Tourist Information Centre, and they will happily tell you about the newly opened wetlands near the jetty which are dedicated to small birds called Latham's Snipe, annual visitors who like Milang so much they fly all the way from Japan.

The clank of cream and milk cans is long gone from Milang's now-rusting butter factory in the main street, Daranda Terrace. Much of its supply came across the lake from Narrung, and it went all the way to winning prizes for butter in London. The town's commercial heart is quiet now, too. Where the butcher once hung sides of lamb out the front, now the Old Butcher Shop B&B verandah looks out to the 1850s Lake Hotel and general store.

In its heyday, Milang was one of the busiest inland ports. Nowadays it's one of the quietest river towns but, be warned, on the Australia Day long weekend it is inundated with yachties as it's the starting point for one of the largest freshwater sailing classics in the world. The rest of the time it's a wonderful little holiday spot on the quiet side of the Fleurieu and it's only 73 kilometres from Adelaide via the South Eastern Freeway and Mount Barker.

Daranda Terrace, Milang
South Australia 5256
Open weekends and public holidays
11 am to 4 pm
Pick up a Heritage Map
from the Post Office on weekdays

Milang Tourist
Information
Centre
Railway Station

The Wharf, Goolwa
South Australia 5214
Tel (08) 8555 34 88
Open daily 9 am to 5 pm
Web www.visitalexandrina.com

Goolwa Visitor
Information
Centre

Raywood Nursery at Cape Jervis

97 km south-west of Adelaide

with Ron Kandelaars

FLEURIEU PENINSULA

Deep Creek Conservation Park is a stunning combination of coastal heath and majestic stringybark forest, and as you drive through the dappled light under the trees you get a sense of what this part of coastal South Australia must have looked like before the farmers and loggers moved in.

At the Raywood Nursery tucked away on the park's outskirts near Delamere you get to walk amongst some of the most ancient stringybark forest in the state. The bush was logged in the 1930s and the timber used in the Broken Hill mines. The unsuitable trees were left behind along with the native grass trees, or Xanthorrhoea. And thank goodness because, according to the nursery owner, Quentin Wollaston, some of them are about 1000 years old.

Quentin showed us the pellets of gum or sap oozing from the Xanthorrhoea trees that were harvested during the Depression to make shellac, a furniture stain. It was also used to make explosives during the war.

The spectacular native grass trees were left behind – thankfully Photo by Quentin Wollaston

It's not surprising that Quentin really knows his stuff, after all he's the grandson of Tullie Cornthwaite Wollaston, a man who left his mark on South Australia's horticultural scene. 'T.C.', as he was known, helped establish the Claret Ash – the tree that provides the wonderful fiery colours in the Adelaide Hills during autumn.

According to Quentin, T.C. found a strange wine-coloured seedling in 1925. He planted the mutant seedling, grew it on and made the first commercial sale four years later. The Claret Ash is now known around the world for its explosive autumnal tones and has even been placed on the National Trust's Heritage Icons list.

T.C.'s zeal for propagating new plants has been inherited by his grandson. At Raywood Nursery, Quentin has successfully grafted a beautiful prostrate flowering blue gum. Normally it would grow several metres high but his plant is virtually a ground cover.

He says part of his success is replicating nature. 'If it means covering the seeds with leaf litter for six months and waiting – that's what we do.' That's the sort of love and care for which Raywood is known and it's a nursery of which old T.C. Wollaston would be proud.

To get to Raywood Nursery take the main road to Cape Jervis and turn left at the Delamere Store. Turn right onto Three Bridges Road and follow the signs. It's open daily.

Tapanappa Road, Delamere
South Australia 5204
Tel (08) 8598 0267
Open daily 9 am to 5 pm

Raywood
Nursery

Water into Wine Tour

83 km south of Adelaide

with Ron Kandelaars

The upper deck offers a better view

It's early morning at the Hindmarsh Island Marina and Peter Summerton fires up the *Wetland Explorer* for another cruise through the lower reaches of the Murray River. Peter and his wife, Jo, regularly take tours through the Tauwitcherie Barrage into the Coorong and on to the Murray Mouth but today we're bound for a special lunch stop at a little-known waterway upstream from Goolwa – the Finniss River.

We motor past the old 1905 paddle-steamer *Oscar W* moored at the Goolwa wharf – a reminder that this part of the river was once a thriving commercial centre with a constant flow of paddlesteamer traffic. With the Hindmarsh Bridge behind us Peter opens the throttle and the *Wetland Explorer* makes up time. It's not long before we lose ourselves in the hidden upper reaches of the Finniss. We glide through a maze of reeds and waterways reminiscent of scenes in the famous Hollywood movie *African Queen*. Some of our fellow passengers even take their drinks onto the *Wetland Explorer*'s upper deck and imitate Katherine Hepburn as they sit back and sip their wine.

According to Peter not many people venture this far up the river because it's very shallow. 'Boats with draughts in excess of three feet quickly find themselves getting stuck.' He also explains that the area was important to Ngarrindjeri people. They used the reeds to make baskets and the 40 or so varieties of fish were an important food source.

Currency Creek Winery

Soon the water peters out and the dairies and vineyards begin to dominate – we've gone as far as we can on our boat leg of the Water into Wine Tour so we change our mode of transport and hop on a bus for a ten-minute ride to the Currency Creek Winery.

While we enjoy some tasting and lunch it becomes clear that the winery has been careful to keep its links with the Murray. The bar is built from the original blocks used in barrage number six which separates the salt from the fresh water down river. The top of the bar is a made from a Norfolk Island pine tree that was chopped down in Victor Harbor.

The emphasis on the lunch menu is local produce – local wine, local food including some delicious yabbies, all enjoyed in front of a wonderful open fire – the perfect setting on a winter's day.

After lunch, there's more tasting and a tour of the nearby Ballast Stone Winery, then back on the *Wetland Explorer* for another backwater tour, this time through Currency Creek on the way home. It's a wonderful way to explore the waterways at the end of the Murray and enjoy some local hospitality in the process.

Coorong Cruises
The Marina, Hindmarsh Island
South Australia 5214
Tel (08) 8555 1133
Email peternjo@esc.net.au
Web www.coorongtours.com.au

Water into
Wine Tour

Willunga Quarry Market

44 km south of Adelaide

with Keith Conlon

FLEURIEU PENINSULA

Whoever said money can't buy you happiness was obviously shopping in the wrong market. The good folk of Willunga must have a particular sense of well being because they have two markets, both of which offer bargains or a very enjoyable browse that costs nowt! There's the weekly Willunga Farmers' Market which is a cornucopia of Fleurieu Peninsula produce and then there's the much bigger and much older sister market over the road – the Willunga Quarry Market.

This market has been gathering the clan on its non-profit community village green since 1986, and on the second Saturday of each month the Southern Expressway brings a new wave of customers. It only takes 45 minutes from town to reach the stalls in the middle of a heritage town that overlooks a sprawl of vineyards and almond orchards.

As you would expect, there is a local flavour among the multicoloured tent stalls. From one row wafts a tempting aroma. 'What's cooking?' I asked, as Pauline stirred the mystery recipe in a tailor-made trailer-stall. 'Sugared almonds from our Willunga block,' she smiled. 'All the better for being cooked by a third generation almond grower.'

With one stall visited there are only 70 or 80 to go! A little further along Jan touches up her beautiful display of potted cyclamens. One of these would go well in the bathroom with a selection of Sandra's 'Greenleaf' hand-made soaps that come in natural fragrances – even Turkish Delight!

Next door is another Willunga Quarry Market original. The six-way body wrap is a shawl-type garment made in Adelaide,

There's plenty of variety

designed and demonstrated at the drop of a hat by the ever cheerful Corina. 'You can slip it over your head like this on a cold day and it will keep you nice and warm.' She managed to hold the game show smile for our camera just an instant before we all dissolved in laughter.

There is a very popular performer who was been conjuring magic tricks at the market for years. Ray Hopwood gathers a crowd as we turn up to see his three ropes of different lengths mysteriously become the same as each other. His patter delights all in the audience and he'll happily sell you a three-rope set with instructions. But don't expect it to work quite so effortlessly first time, after all he's had twenty years' practice.

The old gum trees and grazed hillsides create a rustic backdrop to the market that encourages an ambling pace. Perhaps that's why Agnetta and her spinning wheel are always in one corner adding a timeless vignette as well as a chance to buy a warm and earthy hat and scarf. Asked how much was needed for a jumper, she estimated about $20 worth of wool and eight or ten hours to knit it.

There is a lot of self-expression and personal passion about this market. As we paused for a coffee, a young singer-songwriter performed his own work while teenage music student Bonnie busked on her violin.

If you like talking to collectors, want something handcrafted or grown with loving care and you enjoy country air, this is it. It is what keeps the regulars – customers and stall-holders – coming back month after month.

Willunga Recreation Park
Aldinga Road, Willunga
South Australia 5172
Open second Saturday every month
9 am to 1 pm
Entry free
PO Box 147, Willunga
South Australia 5172

Willunga
Quarry Market

Next to Alma Hotel, Willunga
Every Saturday 8 am to 1 pm
Free entry
Tel (08) 8556 4297

Willunga
Farmers'
Market

Willunga Walks and Talks

44 km south of Adelaide

with Keith Conlon

The founders of the Willunga Quarry Market back in the 1980s wanted to bring people into their heritage town to tarry a while. This idea is now working beautifully with the Willunga Walks and Talks group launched early in 2003.

An enthusiastic volunteer guide like Bev Egel picks up interested market-goers from the information tent and heads off into town, this time with *Postcards* tagging along. We walked up Willunga's main street where the slate footpaths and roofs are evidence that in the 1860s and 70s Willunga's several slate quarries exported thousands of tonnes of slate all over Australia.

At the top of the town, past handsome hotels, former churches and old shops, is the immaculately restored old Post Office and Telegraph Station built in 1857. Bev tells the sad story of Henry Pownsett, one of the first postmasters who, after 32 years and at the

The old Post Office and Telegraph Station Photo by Andrew Strout

Bangor Slate Quarry Photo by Andrew Strout

age of 82, was told to retire. 'He went to his bed and died ten days later.'

Detouring to admire a pretty creek-side cottage called 'Upalong', we were steered down a lane to another gem. 'In 1862 Mr James Bailey Bassett established this school room for boys,' Bev explained, adding that he and his wife had previously run a boarding school next door. Later it was a Council Chamber, and now it's in the hands of the National Trust.

After taking in a host of houses and cottages, shops, trades, churches and more, the tour ends where Willunga's substantial heritage collection is preserved. We arrive at the post-and-rail fenced Government Reserve at the bottom of Willunga Hill where the historic courthouse, police station and stables are now thankfully open to all as the National Trust Museum.

It's the natural base for the Willunga Walks and Talks and combining them with the Willunga Quarry Market at the opposite end of High Street is a fun and interesting way to spend a Saturday in one of our prettiest country towns. It is all coming together very sweetly in Willunga.

Departs Farmers Market every Saturday from 10.30 am
Departs Quarry Market every second Saturday of the month
Departs Old Courthouse and Police Station Museum,
Sunday 10.30 am and 2.30 pm
61 High Street, Willunga
Cost includes entry voucher to the Museum
Bookings essential (08) 8556 2195

Willunga Walks and Talks

Main Road, McLaren Vale
South Australia 5171
Tel (08) 8323 9944

McLaren Vale and Fleurieu Visitor Centre

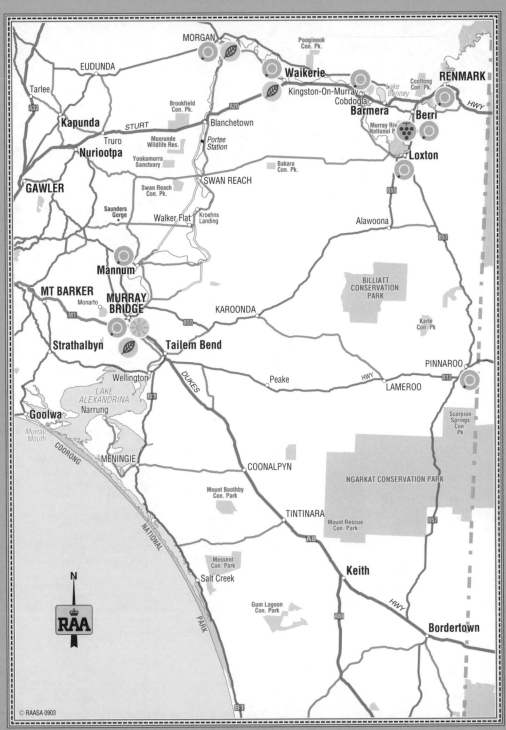

PS *Marion*, Mannum

The River Murray region represents the extremes of the South Australian experience – from the vastness of the river to harsh mallee country.

The Murray River conjures up images of plenty of sunshine, fresh air and fresh produce: brilliant green orchards decorated with vibrant oranges and lemons, thousands of hectares of wine grapes, overflowing crates of stone fruits and nuts – all of which can usually be bought fresh from friendly roadside stalls.

Then there's the 'big river' – towering cliffs, ancient red gums, soaring pelicans, lazy houseboat holidays, historic paddlesteamers and tracts of rugged mallee country. The Murray and its surrounds abound with day trips. Set off early and explore the walking, driving and four-wheel-driving trails of the mallee. Have lunch at Pinnaroo and marvel at the determination of the locals who have carved out a living growing wheat and barley.

Stick to the river and discover the past. Fish under the bridges at Murray Bridge, visit the birthplace of the paddle steamer era at the Mannum Port Dock Museum or experience the river and its wildlife from water-level on a romantic cruise.

See for yourself why the Murray has drawn so many artists and environmentalists. The backwaters, food and wine add to the flavour. But we're not the first to enjoy its magic – the Nguat Nguat Conservation Park near Swan Reach bears proof that Aborigines have been camping on the river's banks and fishing its waters for millennia.

The River Murray experience is a spectacular one and it's right on Adelaide's doorstep.

Tips from the Crew

• Jeff recommends enjoying a drink or meal at one of the many pubs overlooking the Murray River. But don't forget to take your camera – sunset on the river can be spectacular.

• Keith reckons one of the best ways to see the birdlife on the Murray is to book an eco-cruise or hire a kayak and paddle the backwaters.

• Ron recommends Old Tailem Town at Tailem Bend for a glimpse of colonial history. There are more than 90 buildings representing our pioneering past.

• If you are a keen golfer Lisa says the Riverland is the place to head. Berri, Barmera, Waikerie, Loxton and Renmark all have first-class courses.

• Trevor says Olivewood Homestead at Renmark is worth a visit. It's the original home of the Chaffey brothers who pioneered the area's irrigation system and turned the Riverland into South Australia's food bowl.

• Brenda says rose lovers should head to Renmark between September and July when the main street is flushed with rose blooms. A nine-day rose festival is held in October.

Top Attractions

Monarto Zoological Park

Go on one of the popular bus safaris to see giraffes, zebras, cheetahs, rhinoceros and more. The park is a blend of conservation, national and zoological parks.

The Bunyip at Murray Bridge – Sturt Reserve

Discover or rediscover the Bunyip – a childhood institution. You'll tremble with fear or laughter as the memories come flooding back.

Houseboats

Hire a houseboat and cruise the Murray. Boats range from budget to luxury and can cater for as many as 12 passengers. No special licence is required, just a full car licence – tuition is given prior to departure.

Federation Walking Trail

Serious walkers should consider the 58 kilometre trail that starts in Murray Bridge. It traverses the south-eastern Mount Lofty Ranges, winding its way through diverse countryside to a secluded place known as Diggers Rest, near Harrogate. The trail passes historic railyards, river wetlands, rugged gorges, forests, vast farming lands and the Monarto Zoological Park.

Take a Ferry

Travel across the river on one of the 24-hour free ferries located at Wellington, Mannum, Purnong and Swan Reach.

Picnic Time

Enjoy a picnic on the banks of the Murray River. Most towns have excellent lawn areas, complete with public facilities and picnic tables.

Want More Information?

SA Visitor and Travel Centre
1300 655 276

Riverland Hotline
1300 657 625

Riverland website
www.riverland.info

Mannum Visitor Information Centre
(08) 8569 1303

National Parks and Wildlife SA
(08) 8576 3690

RAA Touring (maps and guides)
(08) 8202 4600

SA Tourism Commission website
www.southaustralia.com

Postcards website
www.postcards-sa.com.au

I Didn't Know That

• The historic Randell Dry Dock at the Mannum Dock Museum was once the only dry dock in Australia.
• Wellington became the first crossing point on the Murray in 1836 – the same year as the Colony of South Australia was proclaimed.

• Goolwa was originally known as Port Pullen and was surveyed in 1853.
• In 1954 an 84 kilometre pipeline was completed between Mannum and Adelaide to pump water from the Murray to Adelaide reservoirs.
• The Murray River National Park, south of Berri, is home to over 140 bird species.

• Following the bombing of Darwin in 1942, the Renmark Hotel played a pivotal role in the defence of the Riverland. An air spotter's tower was erected on top of the pub and volunteers scanned the skies for signs of Japanese attack.

Captain Proud Riverboat

78 km
south-east
of Adelaide

with
Ron
Kandelaars

The riverboat PB *Captain Proud* looks like she'd be equally at home on the River Murray or the Mississippi in the days when paddlesteamers were plying their trade up and down these two great rivers. But looks can be deceiving – despite the massive side-wheels there's not a puff of steam in sight.

In fact, the *Captain Proud* is less than 20 years old and is powered by a diesel engine. She used to be The Showboat on the Port River but she's now back at Murray Bridge under the command of skipper Peter Hunter.

We climbed aboard and joined the passengers being well fed on a diet of scones and tea and local history via the Skipper's commentary. As we set out Peter told us the area was originally known as Edward's Crossing after the family who owned the safest crossing point. 'The Edwards family used a barge to transport goods back and forth across the river and they used to swim the cattle across.'

We cruised under an old bridge that Peter says was the first to be built over the river.

Looks can be deceiving – the *Captain Proud* is only 20 years old

The *Dragon Fly* offers a different Murray experience

In 1879 it was one of the biggest engineering projects in the state. 'The river is about 80 feet deep at this point so they had divers in old bell-type diving helmets working on the foundations,' Peter said.

A single controller used to work in the nearby historic Roundhouse coordinating road, rail and animal traffic across the single span. By 1925 a second bridge was carrying the rail traffic and the town became known as Murray Bridge.

As we cruised past the towering cliffs along the river we were given a choice – indulge in another scone on board the *Captain Proud* or hop aboard the *Dragon Fly* for a totally different Murray experience. *Dragon Fly* is a smaller, flat-bottomed boat which takes you right into the Riverglades wetlands, three kilometres upstream from Murray Bridge.

Years ago, much of the land was used for grazing when the water level dropped in summer – now it's a community run wetland that is an important bird rookery. Soon we were gliding through the specially dug channels past pelicans and cormorants who were making the most of partly submerged fence posts.

It's a great way to explore the wonders of the River Murray and see just how fragile the mighty waterway really is. Cruises on both the *Dragon Fly* and the *Captain Proud* depart from the Murray Bridge Wharf but you'll need to book.

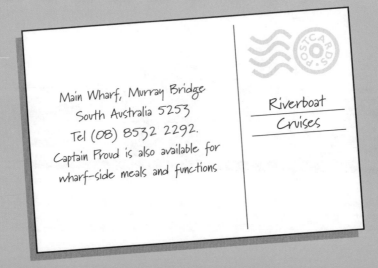

Main Wharf, Murray Bridge
South Australia 5253
Tel (08) 8532 2292.
Captain Proud is also available for
wharf-side meals and functions

Riverboat
Cruises

Garry Duncan, Artist

210 km
north-east
of Adelaide

with
Ron
Kandelaars

The *Postcards* team has had an ongoing love affair with the Murray River and when you spend time on Australia's longest waterway it's not hard to see why. From dawn until dusk the colours and mysteries of this ancient river cast their spell – especially on those who take up the challenge of trying to capture it on canvas.

One such artist is Garry Duncan who believes he has an affinity with the river. He says it has become part of his family so it's not surprising he starts most days taking in the view of the river from the balcony of his Warragai studio near Kingston-on-Murray.

Garry Duncan is passionate about the Murray

Artist and self-described ecologist and activist, Garry says he feels obliged to paint the river in its 'best light' to let everyone know how precious it is. His paintings are vivid and intense and he doesn't shy away from the bold use of colour.

While his paintings reflect the Murray in its most positive light there's a disturbing undercurrent to much of his work. 'I've lived here for thirty years and the place has declined dramatically. We've lost a lot of species, particularly water birds and fish. I haven't seen a tiger snake for probably twenty-five years,' Gary explains. 'The trees are dying, people are taking too much water out and we're too greedy. Greed makes us stupid so we can't see what we're doing.'

A. Humms Ancestral Lands by Garry Duncan

Garry's the sort of bloke who tells it like it is but there's still a touch of the mystic in this artistic bushie. Whether he's in a tinnie searching for new angles along the river cliffs or painting murals on the bridges at Berri and Hindmarsh Island, he's never far from the water.

'Our waterways are vital to our survival. If we disturb the balance the whole thing collapses,' Garry warns. It's a balance he emphasises in all his work.

Warragai Studio, Kingston-on-Murray
South Australia 5331
Viewing appointments
can be made by email.
Email grduncan@riverland.net.au
Web www.garryduncangenius.com

Garry Duncan

Glendower Gallery at Renmark

256 km
north-east
of Adelaide

with
Ron
Kandelaars

RIVER MURRAY

On the main road leading into Renmark from Adelaide there's a wonderful old rambling homestead called Glendower. Out the back is an old fruit packing shed, a reminder that the house was once the centre of a major fruit plantation established in the 1880s not long after brothers George and William Chaffey created the irrigation scheme that turned the countryside into some of the most productive in the country.

Glendower is generally a peaceful place – it was the day the *Postcards* team was there. That is until owner Chris Pearce started his chainsaw and set to work on what looked like a tired, clapped-out piece of pepperwood. To escape the noise we went inside Glendower Gallery and soon discovered what Chris can do with a slab of old wood.

The gallery is full of furniture – all hand-made by Chris and his son, Thom, from materials collected locally. There's nothing this father and son team likes more than wandering through old Riverland sheds uncovering things they can incorporate into their next piece. Like the remains of an old wagon wheel that has been cleverly fashioned into the surround of a dressing table mirror. 'It's the old story – one person sees firewood, a farmer sees a post, and I look at it and see a piece of furniture,' explains Chris.

Part of a wagon wheel frames the mirror

Photo by Jeff Clayfield

The Captain's desk Photo by Jeff Clayfield   Chris and Thom at work Photo by Jeff Clayfield

In a way the works are a repository of Riverland history – every piece has a story and whoever buys that piece gets that story. There's plenty of history in the making too – Chris and Thom are fourth and fifth generation furniture makers. Another feature of their work is the combination of various types of wood – like the hall stand Chris showed us. It had a red gum top, recycled jarrah legs and incorporated old apricot trays from the area's early fruit-growing era.

Then there's the Captain's desk – the top is made from a pepperwood tree planted by William Loxton, one of the Riverland's early boundary riders, after whom Loxton was named. Chris says it's all about retaining some of the region's fast disappearing heritage. Something he and Thom do well through their creative and very original style of furniture.

Cnr 28th Street and
Sturt Highway, Renmark
South Australia 5341
Open daily from 10 am to 4 pm,
or by appointment
Tel 0418 832 132
Web www.riverland.net.au/~dr-bob/

Glendower
Gallery

POSTCARDS

Mallee Tourist and Heritage Centre at Pinnaroo

243 km east of Adelaide

with Ron Kandelaars

D rive east from Murray Bridge and you're soon in the very heart of the South Australian mallee. It's harsh and uncompromising country and like a lot of the state it's been through tough times in recent years with drought and heart-breaking dust storms. But despite the hardship, the tenacity of the locals has prevailed. That's especially true of the people who helped open up this part of the state by establishing wheat and barley farms.

The best way to understand their determination is to visit the Mallee Tourist and Heritage Centre in Pinnaroo. It houses a number of collections that reflect the area's enduring past, including the Gum Family Collection – put together by Don Gum, an old Pinnaroo cockie.

The day the *Postcards* team called in we were lucky enough to meet Don. He's a

The Heritage Centre is crammed with the Mallee's farming past Photos by Max Wurfel

national treasure himself, having received an Order of Australia for community service, and it was great having him show us around the collection that represents the decades he spent on the land. He recollects ordering a John Deere tractor after World War II. 'It took two years to arrive from the United States because of the rationing … and when it did it had doubled in price!'

Don started up an old hand winnower used to separate the wheat from the chaff and he told us to listen carefully. 'You'll hear it sing. Not a song but the tune: "A pound a week and keep, a pound a week and keep, a pound a week and keep".' He was right, the machine did seem to play the tune and Don explained that the winnower operator could expect to 'reap and keep a pound in wages a week'.

It's just one piece in Don Gum's huge collection. He's resisted lucrative offers in the past because he's determined to keep as much of the Mallee's heritage in the Mallee. The collection pays tribute to blokes like the Smith Brothers and their stump jump plough, a classic example of Aussie ingenuity. There's also a replica of the first Ridley Stripper which was built in 1843 and was the first mechanical harvester in the world.

It's just one of 1500 exhibits in the Gum Family Collection on show at the Mallee Tourist and Heritage Centre. The centre also houses a fascinating Letterpress Printing Museum which gives a great insight into newspaper work before computers. There's also the Wurfel Grain Collection – one of the world's biggest collection of grains, it contains more than 1000 varieties and was compiled by another Mallee 'national treasure', the late Donald Wurfel.

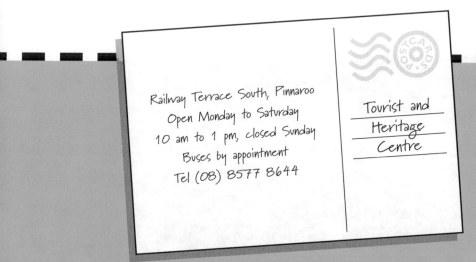

Railway Terrace South, Pinnaroo
Open Monday to Saturday
10 am to 1 pm, closed Sunday
Buses by appointment
Tel (08) 8577 8644

Tourist and
Heritage
Centre

Loxton Historical Village

256 km
east of
Adelaide

with
Lisa
McAskill

There's always something to see   Photo by Allan Hucks

The river town of Loxton was once a regular stop for paddlesteamers which would take on cargoes of wheat grown by the predominantly German settlers who farmed the land in the district. The town was named after William Charles Loxton, a boundary rider who lived beside the river from 1878. His original pug and pine hut has been recreated next to a peppercorn tree he planted on the banks of the Murray.

It now belongs to the local Council and when the *Postcards* team visited, I was delighted to discover it is part of an extraordinary community-based project called the Loxton Historic Village, which has been a tourist drawcard for 30 years.

The village is a fascinating re-creation of how the pioneers lived, especially between 1890 and 1939. It has more than thirty restored and furnished buildings along the main street and as I strolled around I couldn't help wondering about the stories behind the

The Nissen hut when first built Photo by Allan Hucks

buildings – like the original Bank of Adelaide that came from the Mallee town of Geranium. The General Store was salvaged from nearby Alawoona and another cottage from an early residential area of Loxton. The Institute Hall smelled of the linseed oil used to polish the floor.

The faces of Loxton's history look down from the walls on a time warp where the bakery ovens still produce mouthwatering aromas, where sheep are shorn and stationary engines idle smoothly.

The people behind this story are the 50 or so volunteers who breathe life into the historic village. Like the caretaker Jeff Schiller who drives one of the two restored fire engines and volunteer President Allan Hucks who, in retirement, has returned to something he learnt as a teenager – blacksmithing.

You can get a real feel for what it must have been like on one of the early fruit blocks. The drying racks, cutting shed, dipping tank and the basic living conditions in the Nissen Hut paint a vivid picture.

The Loxton Historic Village is open seven days a week and so-called 'Alive Days', when the volunteers dress in period costumes, are held several times a year.

Scenic Road, Loxton
South Australia 5333
Tel (08) 8584 7194
Open Monday to Friday
10 am to 4 pm,
weekends and public holidays
10 am to 5 pm

Loxton
Historical Village

Mallee Fowl Restaurant at Berri

235 km
north-east
of Adelaide

**with
Lisa
McAskill**

RIVER MURRAY

The Mallee Fowl Restaurant is set in mallee scrub off the Sturt Highway near Berri. Just as the native mallee fowl collects leftover and discarded materials to make its rambling nest, so too do Caryl Michael and her husband, Howard.

Inside the restaurant an amazing array of knick-knacks collected over a lifetime hang from the rafters of the barn-like building. Among the 'treasures' I spotted a set of buffalo horns, a toy bi-plane built as a fundraiser for the Royal Flying Doctor Service and even the grille from an early Ford truck.

Howard pointed out that there's quite an art to collecting. He reckons it takes years to refine the art of seeking out and acquiring such highly prized items. I got the distinct impression he had his tongue firmly in his cheek!

For Caryl life at the Mallee Fowl Restaurant is the culmination of a dream which began in 1993 over a campfire in the scrub. 'We were sitting around the

Caryl and Howard – country music fans

Photo by Jeff Clayfield

Carved out of the mallee Photo by Jeff Clayfield

fire with a flask of wine and a book of Banjo Patterson poems. We said what a wonderful spot this is – we ought to build a restaurant.' So they did. Howard and a mate built the place from scratch and it's now a local icon, being declared Australia's Number One Theme Restaurant in 2002.

The Mallee Fowl Restaurant is also a haven for devotees of country and western music. In fact, you'll often find Howard and Caryl entertaining the diners with their guitar and vocal duo. At other times there's a good old fashioned hoedown in an outside amphitheatre. Caryl spent months of back-breaking work carting rocks to build terraces around an old quarry on the site. They now call it The Nest – another reference to the mallee fowl's amazing ability to build a nest far bigger than itself. It's a popular spot for diners who like to sample some real Aussie camp oven cooking.

The restaurant has become a must for locals and visitors to the Riverland as Caryl cooks up a storm on the open grill which, like the music, takes centre stage in the middle of the room. Howard's makeshift cellar in an old concrete water tank provides an endless supply of local Riverland reds.

The Mallee Fowl Restaurant is open for lunch and dinner from Wednesday to Saturday or by appointment. The amphitheatre often hosts live bands and is the main venue for the annual Riverland Country Music Festival each June.

Sturt Highway, Berri
South Australia 5343
Look for the sign near
the Big Orange
Tel (08) 8582 2096

The Mallee
Fowl Restaurant

RIVER MURRAY

PS Mayflower at Morgan

165 km
north-east
of Adelaide

with
Lisa
McAskill

PS *Mayflower* – South Australia's oldest paddlesteamer

Morgan is a quiet and peaceful holiday town these days, but the two grand hotels, the magnificent old shipping agent's warehouse, the Landseer building and the restored wharf are proof that it was once the busiest port in South Australia. Drop into the old railway station museum for a glimpse of what life was like in the 1880s when men were working 24-hour shifts on the wharf and there were six freight trains a day.

But my real *Postcards* assignment was to sample the adventure and romance of life on the water. And I didn't have to look far – moored at the wharf is a charming paddlesteamer, the PS *Mayflower*. She was commissioned in 1884 and is the oldest paddlesteamer in the state. It didn't take much to convince owner Captain Brice Douglas to stoke up the firebox and take us for a cruise. He's passionate about the *Mayflower* and as he cast off he was eager to share the place it holds in the river's history. 'The *Mayflower* was built for a legendary man named Daniel Alexander, or Black Alex to his mates and his enemies,' Brice said.

Black Alex was from the West Indies and a big man – it's claimed he was the strongest on the river. 'He could pick up and carry half a tonne of iron. He also had a reputation for being the best talker on the river – and the best swearer. A colourful character in every sense of the word.'

As we got up steam, Brice showed me the continuous map stored on wooden rollers on a bench in the wheelhouse. He explained that the early riverboat captains used to hand-draw their charts on a length of linen and as they moved along the river they'd scroll the map along to keep track of their location. Brice's map was well worn – complete with cigarette burns and water stains – the early boats didn't have any windows so the maps would get wet when it rained.

The *Mayflower* was known as a 'dew runner', able to glide on water just eighteen inches deep. That meant she could trade on rivers like the Lachlan and the Murrumbidgee where the larger paddlewheelers couldn't operate. But Black Alex's days as a backwater entrepreneur were numbered when the banks moved in. According to Brice they chased him down the Darling and eventually caught him at Wentworth. 'There was one of the biggest fights ever recorded on the river – iron bars and everything as they tried to wrestle the boat from him. The banks won.' Black Alex later worked as a cook on another boat and sadly drowned in the river.

The *Mayflower* continued work as a trader and later as a fishing boat. Brice found her in 1984 and fell in love. She's now fully restored and is permanently moored at the reserve near the ferry. Tours and cruises can be arranged in conjunction with the Morgan Museum. The *Mayflower* is also a feature of Morgan's popular heritage walk which takes in most of the town's landmark buildings and views. You can pick up a brochure and map at the Visitor Information Centre.

Old Railway Station
Riverfront, Morgan
South Australia 5320
Open Tuesday Noon to 4 pm
Or by appointment
Tel (08) 8540 2130

Morgan
Museum

Carmine's Antiques
11 Railway Terrace, Morgan
South Australia 5320
Open Tuesday to Sunday
9 am to 5 pm
Tel (08) 8540 2354

Morgan Visitor
Information
Centre

River Murray Safari

160 km
north-east
of Adelaide

with Lisa McAskill

The MV *Water Rat* can go almost anywhere   Photo by Jeff Clayfield

Just a short paddle upstream from the historic port of Morgan the River Murray makes a sharp detour and heads south to the ocean. The dramatic change in direction at what's called North West Bend was well known to the Overlanders who herded sheep and cattle to South Australia from the eastern states. These days, it's mobs of sightseers being herded to the water's edge by local guide Rex Ellis.

We joined Rex at Weston Flat where we climbed aboard his flat-bottomed boat, the MV *Water Rat*. It can go almost anywhere but we hadn't gone far before we pulled ashore for a closer look at another of the Murray's once booming industries.

We climbed up the cliffs to find a series of dugouts in the heavy clay soil. Rex explained we were walking into what was once a whole community. 'These were wood-cutters' dugouts. They were dug in the early part of last century when the paddlesteamers worked the river.'

Rex reckons the series of holes, alleys and tunnels would have been home to twenty or thirty people. 'A whole family might have lived in one of the little alcoves under a

Rex is at home on the water Photo by Jeff Clayfield

galvanised iron and earth roof,' Rex said. Each day the cutters would head off to fell trees and cut timber to supply the ever-expanding armada of paddle-steamers plying their trade up and down the river.

Rex explained how timber-cutter camps like this were set up at regular intervals along the river bank. Once back on board the *Water Rat* we motored past hundreds of metres of dry-stone wharves built to store and load the wood when the river level was high. Today the area around the dugouts resembles a lunar landscape – proof of how tough the early settlers were to set up home in such an alien environment.

The river is full of surprises and a little further upstream we came across the rusting remains of an old paddlewheel that used to belong to the PS *Randell*. Once a proud river boat she finished her life here as a pumping station. Around another bend we saw an abandoned brandy distillery closed down after being wrecked in the 1956 flood.

The river is full of history and so is Rex. He's also a romantic when it comes to South Australia's waterways and deserts. His Bush Safari Company offers a range of boating, camping, four-wheel-drive and camel riding packages and he'll even take you into the furthest reaches of the Coorong or the Simpson Desert.

P.M.B. 53, Waikerie
South Australia 5330
Tel (08) 8543 2280
Email rexellis@safarico.com.au

Bush Safari
Company

The Mannum Dock Museum

84 km
east of
Adelaide

*with
Keith
Conlon*

The historic river port of Mannum is the birthplace of the famous River Murray paddlesteamer. The historic town buildings are solid proof of the wealth generated by the early days of the river trade and, as we found, a visit to the Mannum Dock Museum gives a wonderful insight into what many consider was a romantic era.

The Museum recounts the period of the original inhabitants, the Ngarrindjeri people, through to the European pioneers who established the river trade. Men like Mannum's founding father, William Randell, who built the *Mary Ann*, the first paddlesteamer on the Murray. Its 'squeeze box' boiler takes pride of place in the Museum. Apparently it heaved and wheezed so much with the build up of stream that chains were wrapped around her … just in case!

Keith at Mannum   Photo by Jeff Clayfield

Mannum is full of stories of the river trade era

Photo by Jeff Clayfield

In 1853 Randell in the *Mary Ann* and Captain Francis Cadell in the *Lady Augusta* set out on separate journeys up river. The Museum displays a wonderful drawing that depicts the great race that followed. After overtaking each other several times, Cadell put in at Swan Hill and Randell continued on to Echuca. Both vessels returned with loads of wool and the river trade was underway.

By the 1860s up to 20,000 bales of wool were being brought down the river each season. The steamers moved huge barges laden with wool. Some continued down the river to Goolwa, others were unloaded at Mannum to be overlanded by bullock teams to Adelaide.

Within a few years the slipway at Mannum was booming. Over 200 paddlesteamers worked the Murray–Darling system. All were shallow draft vessels so they could continue to trade when the river was low.

Next to the Museum is Randell's famous dry dock and the restored 1897 paddlesteamer *Marion*. A cruise on PS *Marion* is an essential part of any visit to this important river trade town. The Mannum Dock Museum incorporates the Mannum Visitor Information Centre so it's well worth a visit to get a handle on this part of the River's attractions.

Randell Street, Mannum
South Australia 5238
Tel (08) 8569 1303
Email mdock@lm.net.au
Open daily
Call to check PS Marion
cruise schedule

Mannum Dock
Museum
(incorporating
the Mannum
Visitor Centre)

Yorke Peninsula

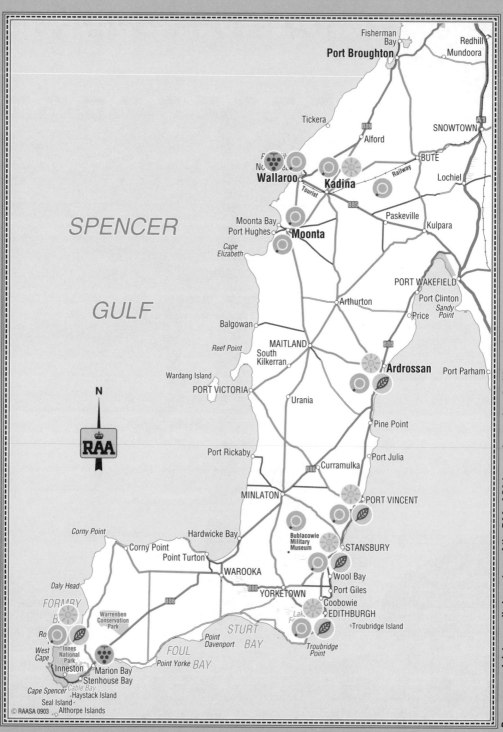

Food/Wine   **Walking/Activity**   **History/Local Interest**   **Nature/Wildlife**

SPENCER

GULF

N

RAA

Fisherman Bay
Port Broughton
Redhill
Mundoora

Tickera
SNOWTOWN

Alford
BUTE
Lochiel

Wallaroo
Kadina
Railway
Tourist
B85
Paskeville
Kulpara

Moonta Bay
Port Hughes
Moonta
Cape
Elizabeth

PORT WAKEFIELD
Port Clinton
Sandy
Point
Arthurton
Price

Balgowan

MAITLAND
Reef Point
South
Kilkerran
Ardrossan
Port Parham

Wardang Island
PORT VICTORIA
Urania
Pine Point

Port Rickaby
Port Julia
B86
Curramulka

MINLATON
PORT VINCENT

Corny Point
Hardwicke Bay
Bublacowie
Military
Museum
STANSBURY

Corny Point
Point Turton
Wool Bay

WAROOKA
Port Giles

Daly Head
YORKETOWN
Coobowie
EDITHBURGH

FORMBY
B.
Warrenben
Conservation
Park
Troubridge Island

Ro
West
Cape
Innes
National
Park
Point
Davenport
Point Yorke
STURT
BAY
Lak
F

Inneston
FOUL
BAY
Troubridge
Point

Cape Spencer
Cable Bay
Marion Bay
Stenhouse Bay
Haystack Island
Seal Island
© RAASA 0903
Althorpe Islands

Base map and data supplied courtesy of the RAA of SA Inc. and reproduced with permission

Port Victoria

Yorke Peninsula is one of the *Postcards* team's favourite day trips. Within ninety minutes of loading our camera gear in the city we can be unpacking it again to film a story on the fascinating mining industry, the ingenuity of the farmers who harvest the land and the sea or the beauty of the peninsula's 600 kilometres of coastline. The Yorke Peninsula has got the lot.

In the north there's the Copper Triangle which takes in Kadina, Moonta and Wallaroo. These towns' history is steeped in the discovery of copper in the 1850s when thousands of miners and their families flooded in from all over the world to seek their fortunes. Climb aboard the Moonta Tourist Train for a novel journey through the mine ruins.

Then there are the historic ports – the towns that grew from the hectic days when ketches and windjammers were shipping grain, wool, salt, gypsum and lime at a frantic rate. Visit the ketch ports on Gulf St Vincent as Keith did on his journey from Edithburgh in the south to Ardrossan further north.

The paddocks are always a patchwork of colour and texture as they bear their annual $300 million grain crop. The surrounding waters also produce world-class seafood for professionals and hopeful anglers, while the beautiful beaches are what holidays on Yorkes is all about.

At the 'tip of the toe' there's Innes National Park offering stunning rugged coastal scenery, hidden beaches, great surfing and fishing, native scrub, heritage accommodation and plenty of wildlife.

As you can see – the list goes on. We always enjoy our trips to Yorke Peninsula and you will too!

Tips from the Crew

• If you are an accomplished surfer Ron suggests West Cape in Innes National Park. It's a left and occasional right-handed beach break up to two metres.

• Lisa says the new boardwalk from Sultana Point to the beach is great. There's disabled access and the floating pontoons are fun for swimmers and boaties. It is just beyond Edithburgh.

• If you visit the Moonta cemetery you'll find the grave of Thomas Woodcock who was poisoned by his wife, Elizabeth. She was the only woman to be hanged in South Australia and was executed in the Adelaide Gaol in 1873.

• Jeff reminds you not to forget your fishing rod as the waters around the peninsula are swimming with King George Whiting, salmon, tommies, snook and squid. Drop your line from one of the many beaches or jetties. If you have time, book a charter boat and make the most of the skipper's local knowledge.

Top Attractions

National Dryland Farming Centre – Kadina

The centre houses one of the biggest collections of farming equipment in the southern hemisphere.

Innes National Park

There are seven walking trails within the park ranging in length from 10 minutes to three hours. Pick up a brochure at the entrance to the park.

Crabbing

Grab a rake and bucket and head for the jetty at Ardrossan to try catching some blue crabs. March and April are the best months.

Geology Trail

At Port Victoria the Geology Trail reveals the ancient volcanic history of the coastline.

Troubridge Island

Take a cruise around Troubridge Island off Edithburgh. It's a Conservation Park and renowned refuge for seabirds. Thousands of birds migrate there each year from Canada, Siberia and Japan.

Food For Thought

Yorke Peninsula is famous for its fresh food. A range of home-made produce like relish, jams and pickles is available at most galleries and craft shops including Harvest Corner Information Centre at Minlaton.

Currency Museum

One of Australia's most unique museums, the Banking and Currency Museum at Kadina has a fascinating display of money and currency. There are more than 2000 moneyboxes and the strongroom is wallpapered with bank notes.

Want More Information?

SA Visitor and Travel Centre
1300 366 770

Yorke Peninsula Visitor Centre – Kadina
1800 654 991

Yorke Peninsula Visitor Centre – Minlaton
(08) 8853 2600

Yorke Peninsula website
www.yorkepeninsula.com.au

National Parks and Wildlife SA
(08) 8854 3200

RAA Touring (maps and guides)
(08) 8202 4600

SA Tourism Commission website
www.southaustralia.com.au

***Postcards* website**
www.postcards-sa.com.au

I Didn't Know That

• Spencer Gulf is a rich prawning fishery and trawlers spend about 80 nights a year collecting their catch.

• Tiny pink and blue orchids and the green and burgundy spider orchids are prolific along the walk from Brown's Beach to Gym Beach at the 'tip of the toe'. Keep an eye out for them in spring.

• Due to a water shortage in 1906, farmers at Ardrossan carted seawater, which was distilled in a huge boiler. In 1914 a pipeline from the Beetaloo and Bundaleer reservoirs was completed and the town had regular fresh supply.

• There are nine shipwrecks lying off Wardang Island near Port Victoria. One of them is the Songvaar, which sank in 1912. She was fully laden with her heavy cargo of 40,000 bags of wheat when she sat on her own anchor, piercing her hull. Strangely, she sank on the same day as the *Titanic*, 14 April 1912.

Bublacowie Military Museum

199 km west of Adelaide

with Ron Kandelaars

A quiet back road on the Southern Yorke Peninsula seems an unlikely place to find a military museum but at Bublacowie, midway between Minlaton and Yorketown, Chris Soar has put together his own tribute to the Australians who have served their country at war.

Chris believes history lives on through his museum. 'Not everyone who went to war laid down their lives – many came back crippled and lost in different ways but they carried on with life. The museum is here to remember everybody who did something for their country.'

The display cabinets are full of photographs, letters and medals representing all branches of the Australian Defence Forces. Much of the memorabilia has strong

The old Bublacowie School is now a moving military museum

All branches of the defence forces are honoured

links with the Yorke Peninsula like the Distinguished Flying Cross awarded to local Ken Keatley. He was from Minlaton and he flew 39 bombing raids over Germany with the RAAF. When Ken died his wife, Doris, asked that his medals be returned to the region he loved so much. Chris says he was very brave: 'One raid over Germany would be enough.'

Chris has seen plenty of action too. He enlisted in the Australian Army in 1962 after emigrating from England. He served in Malaya, Borneo and later as part of the advance party to Vietnam. In peacetime he became a builder – a skill he's used to great effect in retirement having converted the old Bublacowie school into his family home. Some of the children in the early school photos probably played their part in the Australian war effort in World War II. Now they are all part of a moving collection at the Bublacowie Military Museum.

The Bublacowie Campsite right next door can accommodate up to 30 people. Turn off the main road between Minlaton and Yorketown and follow the signs.

Follow signs on
Minlaton–Yorketown Road
Open Sunday, Monday and Tuesday
10 am to 4 pm, closed July
Group bookings by appointment
Contact Chris Soar
Tel (08) 8853 4379

Bublacowie
Military Museum

Innes National Park and Stenhouse Bay

271 km
south-west
of Adelaide

with
Ron
Kandelaars

Innes National Park ranks as one of the most beautiful in the state. It has a spectacular coastline, great fishing – particularly when the mullet are biting at Pondalowie Bay – and at nearby Chinaman's Break surfers match their wits and talent against some monster waves.

All of this helps explain why Innes National Park is one of the most popular parks in South Australia with up to 160,000 visitors a year. In 1970 it was declared a sanctuary for the endangered Western Whip Bird which was rediscovered in the coastal scrub in 1962.

The park has a rich mining history

There's great surfing in the waters around Innes

too. In the 1890s William Innes discovered huge deposits of gypsum and soon the town of Inneston, with its post office manager's house and assorted cottages, was born. The discovery meant the area was protected under a mining lease and saved from the farmers' bulldozers which cleared so much of the rest of Yorke Peninsula.

The gypsum mines also led to the development of Stenhouse Bay at the eastern end of the park. For almost four decades the old beams and planks on the jetty supported a rail cart taking gypsum from an enormous bin at the head of the jetty to the ships bound for Adelaide. Today you can still see the big concrete pylons that supported what was said to be the longest conveyor belt in the southern hemisphere.

The gypsum was mainly used in the building industry, and to this day many old Adelaide villas have plaster ceilings full of gypsum from Yorke Peninsula. Getting ships in and out of Stenhouse Bay in rough weather proved difficult, so in 1932 the Waratah Gypsum Company went to extraordinary lengths to provide a breakwater. The *Hougomont* had been dismasted off nearby Althorpe Island and was eventually scuttled off Stenhouse Bay. But her role as a breakwater was

The Stenhouse Bay Jetty

short-lived – rough seas broke her up and she's now part of the Maritime Heritage Diving Trail.

It's hard to imagine today that the peaceful tourist centre of Stenhouse Bay was once a bustling town supporting nearly 600 people. The jetty and storage bin are reminders of those halcyon days. There are a number of camping grounds within the park and heritage accommodation is available through National Parks. The Park headquarters is also at Stenhouse Bay and a vehicle entry fee applies.

Stenhouse Bay
South Australia 5577
Tel (08) 8854 3200
Open Monday to Friday
9 am to 4.30 pm,
Saturday and Sunday
10.30 am to 2 pm,
holiday weekends
9 am to 4.30 pm

Innes National
Park Visitor
Centre

Innes from the Royston Trail

Kadina – part of 'Australia's Little Cornwall'

146 km
north-west
of Adelaide

with
Keith
Conlon

The pretty town of Kadina proudly carries the title of unofficial capital of the Yorke Peninsula. It's now Yorke's biggest town and commercial hub, but it was originally laid out to serve the giant copper mine that brought thousands of miners and their families all the way from Cornwall.

Kadina celebrates that heritage by joining with nearby Wallaroo and Moonta to make up 'Australia's Little Cornwall'. There's no escaping the mining influence – my visit began at the old copper mine on the town's outskirts. The area was originally a sheep

Headgear like this was common throughout the copper triangle

run but that changed dramatically in 1859 – thanks to a wombat of all things! It seems the wombat was digging among the limestone and threw up some green rocks that were spotted by an observant shepherd.

The discovery of those copper-laden rocks had a dramatic effect. Within a few years there were 2000 men and boys working the giant mine. These days, Harvey's engine house is the last sentinel standing above the lode that ran for more than 500 metres. Local author and historian Keith Bailey took us back in time as he explained how deep the ore body went. 'It took an hour to climb down 1000 feet so if they started work at half past seven, they had to be at the top of the shaft at half past six.'

Keith's grandfather was one of the thousands of Cornishmen to work the mine. He reckons the Cornishmen were the best hard rock miners in the world. 'They used to say whenever you found a hole there'd be a Cornishman at the bottom of it.'

By 1875 there were 20,000 people in the area and most of them were of Cornish origin. Many of the miners lived in humble cottages, some of which are still standing in Kadina.

Giant steam-driven pumps ran 24 hours a day in engine houses like the Harvey to keep the groundwater at bay. The main shaft is now full of water and

Top: Harvey's Engine House Photo by Jeff Clayfield
Bottom: It was hard work below ground

the surface boils with a constant stream of bubbles from deep below. It is a trifle on the nose, too. 'The pong is hydrogen sulphide, or rotten egg gas,' smiled Keith. 'There is a lot of sulphur down the mine, and it is being produced all the time.'

Owner of the mine, former sea captain and pastoralist Walter Watson Hughes, amassed a fortune and his statue sits on North Terrace in front of the University of Adelaide. Before they closed in 1923, the amalgamated Moonta and Wallaroo mines had produced twenty million pounds worth of copper.

Matta House and Heritage Museum

Behind the Kadina Visitor Centre is a real survivor of that fantastic era. Matta House, with its shingle-roof and pickaxe beer bottle borders and cottage garden, is now a quiet insight into domestic life of the late nineteenth century. It was built for the mine manager of the Matta Matta mine. You'll find yourself walking into a beautifully kept family home and, because original Cornish mining families donated much of the furniture and ornaments, it is a real heirloom collection. It's run by the National Trust and is open every day as part of the National Dryland Farming Visitor Centre.

Matta House and its cottage garden are real survivors Photo by Jeff Clayfield

The Wombat Hotel – named after the animal that dug up the first ore Photo by Jeff Clayfield

Historic Walking Tour

Kadina also boasts an hour-long heritage walking tour. Look out for the Royal Exchange Hotel, with its cast-iron lace verandah trimmings and coat of arms above its corner doors. It was built in time to welcome the famous English cricketer W.G. Grace and his touring team in 1874, and not long after, the future King George V dropped in for dinner after visiting the mine.

The mining influence is obvious – the two-storey Kadina Hotel started out as the single level Miners Arms. And the oddly named Wombat Hotel was originally a boarding house. It was named after the animal that dug up the first pile of copper ore.

Cornish Pastie

A visit to Australia's Little Cornwall just isn't complete without sampling a little traditional fare – where better to try the Cornish pastie? A couple of the local bakeries still serve up the oddly shaped creation that has a raised 'plait' of curled pastry from one end to the other.

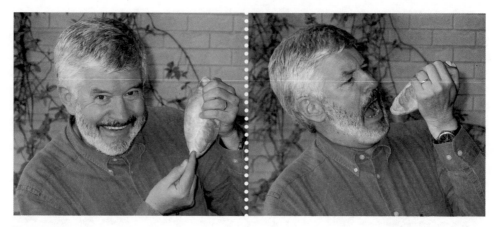

The curled pastry handle really works   Photos by Jeff Clayfield

The pastry cooks confirmed the plait was invented to act as a handle for a hungry miner to grab with his dirty hands. He would eat the meat and veg pastry packet, leaving the nice jam 'dessert' at one end till last, before throwing the pastry curl away. I tried it out during a break in the quaint band rotunda in Victoria Square, and I can assure you it's a good feed.

Little Cornwall even has its own festival – 'Kernewek Lowender' means Cornish happiness and there's always plenty of that during the biennial Cornish Festival. It's a three-day celebration that involves Kadina, Moonta and Wallaroo and is certainly worth a visit. Call the Visitor Information Centre for details.

But you don't have to wait until then, Australia's Little Cornwall is a great destination any time.

incorporates the National Dryland Farming Centre
50 Moonta Road, Kadina
South Australia SA 5554
Tel 1800 654 991
Web www.yorkepeninsula.com.au

Yorke Peninsula
Visitor
Information
Centre

Marion Bay Pizzas

265 km west of Adelaide

with Lisa McAskill

Over the years the *Postcards* team has fallen under the spell of Innes National Park at the bottom of Yorke Peninsula. From the historic old ghost town of Inneston to the shack village at Pondalowie Bay, the park offers many recreational options.

In your travels around what's called 'the tip of the toe' it pays to drop into the Marion Bay Tavern where local seafood features heavily on the pizza menu. The Tavern is owned by Graham Virgin, an ex-surfer who fell in love with the peninsula years ago. Now he and his wife, Robyn, have come up with a few novel additions to the pub. If the wood fire gets out of control they know they can't rely on the rainwater tank because it's now a vital part of the Marion Bay culinary scene – it's the pizza oven.

The rainwater tank now turns out superb pizzas Photo by Ted Dobrzynski

The tavern is the ideal place to take a break Photo by Ted Dobrzynski

The chefs have perfected the art of pizza making. They reckon there's a real art to making dough, especially for wood ovens. After a few impressive twirls in the air, the base gets a liberal layer of tomato sauce, cheese, herbs and marinated seafood including calamari, prawns, baby octopus and finally smoked oysters.

After several minutes cooking in the rainwater tank, hey presto – the seafood special! It's a real hit at the Marion Bay Tavern overlooking the local jetty, and just the trick if you get a little peckish on your travels.

Main Road, Marion Bay
South Australia 5575
Tel (08) 8854 4141
Open daily from 10 am

Marion Bay
Tavern

Maritime Trail

275 km
south-west
of Adelaide

with
Lisa
McAskill

With the relentless surf and rugged coast it's not surprising that the southern tip of Yorke Peninsula is littered with shipwrecks. And as if the waves weren't enough there's the array of islands and reefs to add to the hazards for unsuspecting skippers.

An Interpretive Maritime Trail along the coastline brings to life the tales of bravery and tragedy. Like the story of the Norwegian barque *Ethel* that ran aground on a beach in Innes National Park 1904. She'd sailed from South Africa to pick up a cargo of wheat at Port Adelaide when she was caught in a freak storm and dismasted. She was at the mercy of the wind and waves and the captain asked for a volunteer to swim ashore and raise the alarm. Eighteen-year-old Leonard Stenersen said he'd give it a go and dived into the pounding surf with a security rope attached. He made it to shore only to lose his footing and to be sucked back into the monstrous waves. His mates on board hauled him back to the stricken vessel only to lose him again at the last minute.

The coast around Innes is rugged but beautiful

By daybreak the storm had passed and all except Stenersen walked ashore. For years the wreck of the *Ethel* on Ethel Beach has been a favourite picnic site and a photographer's dream. The superstructure remained intact for decades but the forces of nature have taken their toll. It's now a jumble of rusting iron, but still worth a visit.

Ironically the vessel that raised the alarm when the *Ethel* was in trouble back in 1904 also ran aground sixteen years later. In 1920 the coastal steamer *Ferret* was bound for Port Victoria when she was caught in thick fog. The captain changed course to avoid nearby Althorpe Island and instead crashed into the beach. It was a harrowing experience for the crew but mercifully they all survived.

It certainly caused a stir at Inneston though – the gypsum and salt workers made a bee-line for the beach when they heard part of the *Ferret*'s cargo was bottles of grog and some had washed ashore. Now all that remains of the *Ferret* is its boiler.

The surf is slowly taking its toll on both wrecks. On rough days it's possible to see iron from both ships being tossed around in the waves – an indication of the power of the swell and the size of the waves in this area.

There are a number of other wrecks along the coast and they are popular with divers but you can see the *Ethel* and *Ferret* without getting your feet wet. They are well signposted from the road through Innes National Park and the car park above the beach has a great photographic display of the tragedy, even showing the recovered anchor of the *Ethel*.

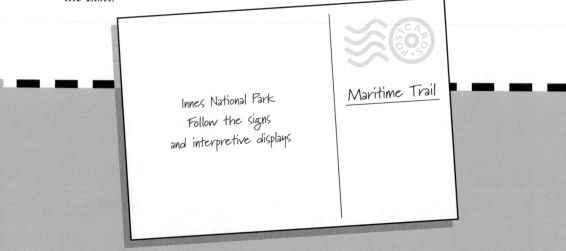

Innes National Park
Follow the signs
and interpretive displays

Maritime Trail

Moonta Mines Railway Tour

167 km
north-west
of Adelaide

*with
Ron
Kandelaars*

All aboard – the tourist train is a great way to see the copper mine site

s we climbed aboard a tiny tourist train it became clear that Moonta's history is in safe hands. Our driver was Trevor Gibbons, the coordinator of a group of enthusiastic and knowledgeable volunteers who operate the National Trust railway that runs through the old copper mine precinct.

As the train moved off Trevor began his commentary about the 1861 discovery of copper by a shepherd called Paddy Ryan. His find led to what became known as the Copper Triangle made up by Moonta, Kadina and Wallaroo.

Within four years there were 1700 men and boys working the mines supporting a town of about 12,000. The train ride reveals a number of simplified but fascinating insights into the copper operation, like the remains of the big tanks that were used to sort the ore. Iron and copper ore were dropped into the tanks that were full of saltwater pumped from the gulf. When the water was drained the copper stuck to the iron and was scraped off, collected and shipped to market via Wallaroo.

The train journey takes 50 minutes

The flushing of the used salt water was blamed for much of the degradation of the bush around the mine sites which, thankfully, through a program of regeneration, is now being reclaimed by native plants. As Trevor pointed out, the revegetation is appropriate because Moonta got its name from a local Aboriginal word meaning 'impenetrable scrub'.

The boom times came to an end in 1923 when the mine closed and with it went much of the population. But Moonta has survived as an agricultural and service centre and through its pride in its heritage. That's illustrated by a stop at the railway station that has been restored and is now the local tourist office.

The train begins and ends outside the National Trust's museum built in the old Moonta Mines School. The 50-minute narrow gauge railway journey departs at various times on weekends and during public and school holidays.

Mines Museum
Verran Terrace, Moonta Mines
South Australia 5558
Tel (08) 8825 1891

Moonta Mines
Railway

Sonbern Lodge at Wallaroo

157 km
north-west
of Adelaide

with
Lisa
McAskill

W hen the rich pastoralist Walter Watson Hughes first took up a lease on Yorke Peninsula in the late 1850s his sheep station was called Wallawaroo. The name proved too long for stencilling on wool bales so it was shortened to Wallaroo.

Sonbern Lodge is one of the grand old buildings of a boom era Photo by Lindsay Weir

Not that Hughes spent too much time worrying about the price of wool – the copper discovered underground made him fabulously wealthy and soon the towns of the Copper Triangle were churning out mountains of copper ingots bound for overseas.

Many of the grand old buildings of that boom era remain including the impressive Coffee Palace and Guest House, which was built in 1912 to accommodate the increasing rail traffic. The Coffee Palace, now known as Sonbern Lodge, was built by William Reece and the scale and workmanship, including its impressive verandahs, speaks of a confidence in the future of Wallaroo. Reece even hired horses and carts to people who wanted to explore the local area.

But that confidence was misplaced – the copper mine closed in 1923 and the area began to decline. For several years during the Great Depression the guest house was closed, but by the late thirties it was back in business offering overnight accommodation to passengers arriving in the town on the train from Adelaide and heading west on the steamers across Spencer Gulf to the Eyre Peninsula.

Today Sonbern Lodge offers heritage accommodation and the chance to sample the history of this famous copper town. You can also call in to pick up a free map of Wallaroo's Heritage Walk.

18 John Terrace, Wallaroo
South Australia 5556
Tel (08) 8823 2291

Sonbern Lodge

Wallaroo Heritage and Nautical Museum

157 km north-west of Adelaide

with Lisa McAskill

As you wander around Wallaroo today you might think little has changed. Ships from across the world still call in to pick up Yorke Peninsula grain from the town jetty, but to really appreciate how the town has evolved, step back in time at the Wallaroo Heritage and Nautical Museum.

Inside you'll see the role copper played in the area's development. According to the Museum's curator, Colin Boase, the best copper in the world was being processed here from the nearby Wallaroo and Moonta mines. He showed us a big copper ingot made at the Wallaroo copper smelters which operated between 1861 and 1923. The ingot was recovered from the sea floor after falling off the jetty while being loaded.

In its heyday more than a thousand men and boys worked at Wallaroo and when you look at the collection of early museum photos you realise environmental issues weren't high on the agenda. According to Colin pollution was at its height in the early 1900s when there were thirteen smelters belching smoke.

The anchor gives a hint of what's inside

By 1923 the last copper smelter had closed but another industry had taken its place. Ships were again queuing at the town but now it was bagged wheat and barley they were taking to Europe.

Many of the majestic sailing ships were owned by Gustaf Erikson in the Aland Islands off the coast of Finland. From the 1920s until as late as 1949 Erikson's fleet of windjammers regularly made the run across the world and around Cape Horn to Spencer Gulf, establishing links between South Australia and Finland. And many of those links live on today at the museum through a number of stunning miniature ships in bottles. Colin showed us an example. 'It was made by one of the cadets during a voyage from Finland to Wallaroo in 1935. He returned to Wallaroo a few years ago and left it on the doorstep.'

Mementos from those epic journeys are scattered throughout the museum and there's a fascinating audio visual display that lets you relive the days when the crews staged races between Wallaroo and their home ports. In some cases the trip was completed in 91 days.

When they weren't racing on the open sea the sailors were holding rowing regattas with the locals. There are a number of photographs depicting the competitions including one of a boat called *The McKee*. In 1935 a crew of local Wallaroo lads took on a crew from the *Abraham Rydberg* and rowed from one end of the jetty to the other.

For the record the locals won and their photos still take pride of place in the Wallaroo Heritage and Nautical Museum.

Jetty Road, Wallaroo
South Australia 5556
Tel (08) 8823 3015
Open Wednesday 10.30 am to 4 pm,
Tuesday, Thursday, Saturday, Sunday
and school holidays 2 pm to 4 pm
Or by appointment

Wallaroo
Heritage and
Nautical Museum.

Tiparra Lighthouse, Wallaroo

Yorke Peninsula Railway

157 km
north-west
of Adelaide

with
Ron
Kandelaars

A trip on the Wallaroo to Bute tourist railway is on the 'must do' list for any train buff. The old 1960s T-class diesel regularly pulls the historic carriages across the top of Yorke Peninsula taking its passengers on a trip back in time. The train rolls past the mine ruins and cottages that were home to the 'Cousin Jacks' and 'Jennies' – the early miners and their wives who made this part of South Australia their own Little Cornwall.

The 140-year-old line has had seven owners and in 1994 it was taken over by a group of volunteers who take great delight in sharing their passion. After leaving Wallaroo, the train heads towards Kadina and on to Bute, and as the scenery slips by there's a sense of the endless procession of the seasons – some good and some bad. The train travels on

The T-class diesel is now run by volunteers

a line that goes back to the days when the first cereal farmers cleared the mallee scrub and established tiny settlements like Willamulka with its 1880s Methodist Church set in a field.

The day we went on the train, we were with a group of local kids on a school excursion. They probably didn't realise it but they were travelling in the squeaky comfort of carriages almost a century older than them. The wood-panelled carriages used to be on The Overland service between Adelaide and Melbourne.

The train used to be the lifeline of the local towns

Up front in the engine, there's no hiding the delight of Kevin Masters, the railway's president who has worked tirelessly to keep the train on track – he's happy to be behind the controls. Kevin knows this line was the lifeblood of towns like Kadina, Wallaroo and Moonta – whether as a horse-drawn gravity line during the 1860s copper boom or in the days when the freight trains picked up bagged wheat and barley from the sidings.

The train departs the historic Wallaroo Station one weekend a month and is a great way to see the northern end of the Yorke Peninsula. There are extra services during school holidays.

Return trip Wallaroo to Bute
For timetable and bookings contact:
Yorke Peninsula Visitor Centre
50 Moonta Road, Kadina
South Australia 5554
Tel 1800 654 991
or (08) 8821 2333

Yorke Peninsula
Railway

Wheal Hughes Mine Tours at Moonta

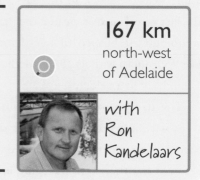

167 km north-west of Adelaide

with Ron Kandelaars

The underground tours are popular

'Wheal' is the Cornish word for mine and it's certainly appropriate for the enormous pit just outside Moonta which circles its way like a corkscrew to the lode below. A visit to the Wheal Hughes helps you understand the role mining played in South Australia's development.

The Wheal Hughes is young compared to the original mines worked by the thousands of Cornishmen in the late 1800s. Western Mining began the Wheal Hughes in 1991 but it only operated for three years before the falling price of copper forced it to close. That was long enough to create a monstrous mine and the journey below ground on one of Alwyn Johns' guided tours is a fascinating experience.

Dressed in hard-hats complete with miner's lamps, Alwyn took us into the giant open cut and at the 65 metre level pointed out the three copper lodes the miners were chasing. From there we entered the portal, or tunnel, and proceeded underground to the largest of the cathedral-like chambers – this one 55 metres below sea level. The copper lode actually runs 95 metres below sea level but, as Alwyn joked, we'd need a submarine to go that low as groundwater appears at the 70 metre mark.

The open cut mine   Blue copper vein

Inside the big chamber you realise how hard even the modern day miners had to work as they manoeuvred their drills into the tight corners chasing the lode. It was heavy, hot and dirty work, but at least they had hydraulic drills and modern equipment – unlike the early miners who used picks and shovels. And to illustrate what it must have been like in those very early days, Alwyn briefly turned off the lights and let our group experience the mine via candlelight. It was certainly an eerie feeling and there were a few sighs of relief when the electric lights came back on.

Alwyn conducts tours daily and it's a great journey through a fascinating part of South Australia's history.

Poona Road
(2.8 kilometres from Moonta
township), Moonta
South Australia 5558
Tel (08) 8825 1892

Wheal Hughes
Copper Mine

Yorke Peninsula's Ketch Ports

with Keith Conlon

These days the romantic old ketch ports on the eastern side of Yorke Peninsula mean sunny seaside holidays and a modern real estate boom. But they were born of plenty of hard yakka on the farms and back-breaking wheat bag stacking on the jetties. They're an easy drive around the top of Gulf St Vincent so the *Postcards* team set out early one day for what promised to be a very pretty trip.

Edithburgh

222 km
west of
Adelaide

We began down at the heel of Yorke Peninsula at Edithburgh where the cliff-top walk on the edge of town offers views of a distant silo to the north, Sultana Point to the south and away on the horizon, tiny Troubridge Island with its own lighthouse. You can take a half-hour boat trip and spend a night or two in the lighthouse keeper's cottage if you want a taste of solitude. But you'll share the experience with thousands of feathered visitors who like it so much they migrate annually from Siberia and Japan.

Edithburgh faces east to Gulf St Vincent and beyond the unusual tidal swimming pool the old jetty was hosting its daily bunch of hopeful anglers. We also watched a pod of scuba divers enjoying the sparkling clear waters around the old wooden jetty piles.

It's all very relaxed now – a contrast to the late 1800s when thousands of tonnes of salt harvested from nearby inland lakes were being shipped through here. Call into the Edithburgh Museum in the old Produce Store in the Main Street to learn about how this largely forgotten industry saved the town. When wheat and barley were planted in the late 1860s the farmers harvested bumper crops. But within a few seasons much of the soil had been depleted of key trace elements and farmers found the going tough.

The ever hopeful anglers on the jetty Photo by Keith Conlon

That is until they began harvesting the salt. The museum depicts the time when 200 lakes kept the Edithburgh salt refineries working overtime and the town's population swelled to 2000 during harvest time.

It was all very prosperous and doubtless a bit noisy in those days when the impressive banks, hotels and guest houses were built along the main street. It's a little more laid back these days but the town is doing very nicely as young and old come to take it quietly.

Edith Street, Edithburgh
South Australia 5583
Tel (08) 8852 6187
Open Sundays, school holidays and
public holidays or by appointment

Edithburgh
Museum

Stansbury

197 km
west of
Adelaide

It was time for us, however, to head north to find the small port town of Stansbury which sits on a spur into the blue waters of Gulf St Vincent. From the cliffs that rise just to the north, we marvelled at the placid, beckoning scene, and concluded that whoever put the caravan park at Oyster Point was onto a good thing. The front row sits on lawns that roll down to a protected sandy beach. Stansbury is a smooth two-and-a-half hours' drive from Adelaide but for a good part of its life, the only way in and out was by sea. The mosquito fleet – hundreds of coastal ketches – brought in the news of the world and took out cargo of all kinds.

In the 1840s the first industry revolved around native oysters which were touted as the best in South Australia. In fact, the town was originally known as Oyster Bay. On the shallow flats today, Stansbury's pacific oyster growers are busily re-establishing that reputation.

Stansbury Jetty protrudes into the blue waters of Gulf St Vincent Photo by Jeff Clayfield

As well as the hundreds of thousands of tonnes of wheat and barley for which the peninsula is still famous, the cargo through the port during the nineteenth century included olive oil, jam from a nearby factory and even wine from a local winery.

The white sandy beach also offered respite from the hot work of lime-burning on the local farms. If your house is more than a few decades old,

A boaties' paradise

there's a chance it's held together with lime shipped from here. The lime was mixed with sand and cement to make mortar. There were fifteen lime-burning kilns in the area and the schooners were taking 2000 bags a week to Adelaide. Keep a lookout for signs to the restored Wool Bay Lime Kiln.

Cnr Weaver and Towler Streets,
Stansbury
South Australia 5582
Tel (08) 8852 4577

Stansbury Visitor
Centre

North Terrace, Stansbury
South Australia 5582
Tel (08) 8852 5020
Open Sunday and Wednesday
2 pm to 4 pm,
open daily in January
Or by appointment

Stansbury
Museum

Port Vincent

181 km
west of
Adelaide

A bit further north, Port Vincent reveals a tale of three centuries. The old town wharf tells of its first life as a ketch port, the beach-side kiosk and boat ramp are part of its holiday town transfor-mation in the twentieth century, and a little further north the earth movers have carved out a twenty-first-century marina.

A stroll from the wharf up the main street takes you past a number of important buildings that were erected about 120 years ago. Among them is the Grain Store which was built by local farmer Joseph Parsons. He pioneered the use of phosphate on crops on the peninsula and improved his yield so dramatically he needed somewhere to store the grain. Come the twentieth century, the building has had many uses. It's earned a place on the State Heritage List because of its central role in Port Vincent's life – as a bank, grocer, gallery, church, post office and coffee shop.

Blue water, blue sky – what more could the day-tripper want? Photo by Keith Conlon

The legendary stump jump plough – invented in Ardrossan Photo by Keith Conlon

Ardrossan

137 km

north-west
of Adelaide

We saved the biggest for last. Ardrossan is the largest Yorke Peninsula ketch port on Gulf St Vincent. The name came from Ayrshire in Scotland, but mercifully not the climate. Ardrossan today means crabbing country, with big blue crabs for the taking for those who know how.

A lone agricultural implement in the clifftop town park is a reminder that Ardrossan is also the home of the legendary stump jump plough that revolutionised farming throughout South Australia's vast mallee regions. Richard Smith and his brother Clarence invented it in 1877, and Ardrossan's fine historical museum is housed in part of the factory that once employed 120 men and turned out fourteen ploughs per week. The town was thriving then, and it is again now.

The two jetties are crucial in Ardrossan's story. The 400 metre port jetty used to carry a horse-drawn tramway out to the mosquito fleet and steamers. In 1926, 200,000 bags of wheat were loaded here. Then came an historic deal that lead to the dual-purpose monster jetty to the south. BHP opened its nearby dolomite mine in 1948 and needed a jetty capable of loading its big ships. Premier Tom Playford agreed to help

The coastline at Ardrossan is stunning

provided it also included bulk wheat loading facilities. As a result, the BHP (now OneSteel) jetty also has what were South Australia's first bulk grain silos that can hold 250,000 tonnes.

No visit to Ardrossan is complete without a trip to the top of the lookout over the mine two kilometres south of the town. It offers a great view of the mine on one side, and of Ardrossan and the gulf on the other.

Fifth Street, Ardrossan
South Australia 5571
Open Sunday and public holidays
2.30 pm to 4.30 pm

Historic Museum
(Stump Jump
Plough)

50 Moonta Road, Kadina
South Australia 5554
Tel 1800 654 991
Email tourism@yp-connect.net

Yorke Peninsula
Regional Visitor
Information
Centre

Wakefield Press and Channel Nine thank the following organisations and individuals for use of their photos in *Postcards: Day trips from Adelaide*.

Keith Bailey, p 118, 119 bottom; Barossa Wine and Tourism, p 33, 34; Colin Boase, Wallaroo Heritage and Nautical Museum, p 131; Chateau Tanunda, p 29, 30; Father Mark Cooper, p 13, 14;

Coorong Cruises, p 81; Currency Creek Estate Wines, p 82; Garry Duncan, p 93, 94; The Encounter Centre, p 71, 72; Sal Hawker, p 47, 48, 49; Peter Hunter, p 91, 92; Pam Jenson, p 83; Colin Liebig, p 32; Lions Club of Yorke Peninsula Rail, p 134, 135; Mount Surmon Winery, p 61, 62; National Trust, Moonta, p 127, 128; Orlando Wyndham, p 35, 36, 37;

Pages Publishing, p 136, 137; Port of Morgan Heritage Society, p 103; SA Tourism, p iv, 1, 4, 5, 6, 19, 23, 25, 26, 43, 46, 51, 54, 59 Top, 63, 66, 76, 87, 89, 90, 109, 112, 115, 117, 132, 141, 144; Enid Soar, p 113, 114; Richard Thomas, NPWS, p 116, 125; University of Adelaide, p 20–21, 22; Wally Wallis, p 58, 59 Bottom

Out 'n' about

Many thanks to the crew and everyone who helps make *Postcards* so successful. Happy touring

The *Postcards* crew and some helpers

Smile Jeff . . .

. . . that's better

Jeff, Keith and Trevor with guide Amy Pysden on Granite Island

Keith and Jeff plan a segment

We get around – Trevor and Jeff on K.I.

The stunning sea views from Granite Island

Happy Trails

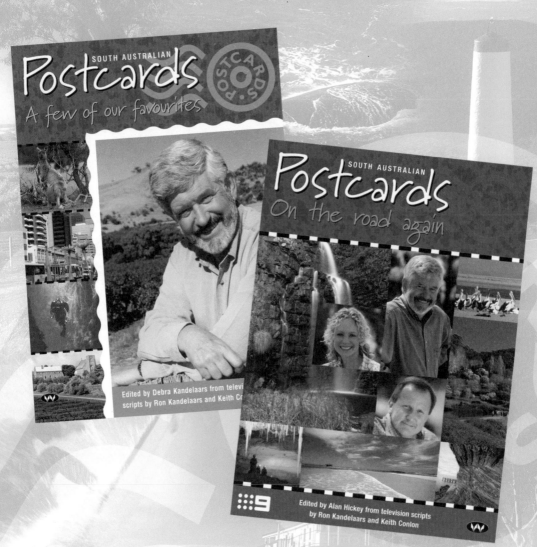

More great reading
from the Postcards crew